Literature in Perspective

General Editor: Kenneth Grose

C. von Nolcken
St Anne's College
Oxford.

Old English Literature

Literature in Perspective

Old English Literature

M. W. Grose and Deirdre McKenna

Evans

Evans Brothers Limited, London

Published by Evans Brothers Limited
Montague House, Russell Square, London, W.C.1

Set in 11 on 12 point Bembo and printed in Great Britain by
The Camelot Press Ltd, London and Southampton
ISBN 0 237 35207 9 cased   PRA 3129
ISBN 0 237 35208 7 limp

Literature in Perspective

Reading is a pleasure; reading great literature is a great pleasure, which can be enhanced by increased understanding, both of the actual words on the page and of the background to those words, supplied by a study of the author's life and circumstances. Criticism should try to foster understanding in both aspects.

Unfortunately for the intelligent layman and young reader alike, recent years have seen critics of literature (particularly academic ones) exploring slender ramifications of meaning, exposing successive levels of association and reference, and multiplying the types of ambiguity unto seventy times seven.

But a poet is 'a man speaking to men', and the critic should direct his efforts to explaining not only what the poet says, but also what sort of man the poet is. It is our belief that it is impossible to do the first without doing the second.

Literature in Perspective, therefore, aims at giving a straightforward account of literature and of writers—straightforward both in content and in language. Critical jargon is as far as possible avoided; any terms that must be used are explained simply; and the constant preoccupation of the authors of the Series is to be lucid.

It is our hope that each book will be easily understood, that it will adequately describe its subject without pretentiousness so that the intelligent reader who wants to know about Donne or Keats or Shakespeare will find enough in it to bring him up to date on critical estimates.

Even those who are well read, we believe, can benefit from a lucid expression of what they may have taken for granted, and perhaps—dare it be said?—not fully understood.

K. H. G.

Old English Literature

Many people meet Old English for the first and only time when they are compelled to read some to 'stiffen' a university English course. Fortunately those days are passing now, for the rudiments of any language rarely make pleasant or representative reading, and compulsion has killed many a budding interest. In these courses, too, to give this stiffening effect the emphasis has had to be more on grammatical niceties and accuracy of construe than on its literary merits.

We believe, however, that it is worth the drudgery of the early stages of learning the language to explore the literature; thus in the first two-thirds of this book we attempt to put it in its setting, and describe its more important monuments. The last third we have devoted to an anthology of our own translations of some of the texts and authors dealt with in the first part. We have been led to this break with the pattern of the series in the hope that by providing a sample conveniently to hand we may encourage others to a desire to explore for themselves what has usually been the preserve of the specialist or conscript.

M. W. G.
D. M. McK.

Contents

The Authors

M. W. Grose is Bibliographer to the Oxford English Diction-
ary Supplement and is author of *Chaucer* in this series. Deirdre
McKenna is an Editorial Assistant with the Oxford English
Dictionary Supplement.

Acknowledgements

The authors and publishers are indebted to the Bodleian Library for the reproduction of the first leaf of Alfred's *Pastoral Care*, and to the Trustees of the British Museum for the cover photograph and the three other illustrations.

I

Prologue: On Reading Old English

Quid Hinieldus cum Christo? What has Ingeld, the hero of Germanic legend, to do with Christ? Or, to rephrase Alcuin's rebuke to the monks of Lindisfarne more colloquially: what are you doing listening to the old pagan lays when you ought to be paying attention to the Bible and the Fathers? The relevance of the question becomes more apparent when we recognise that if clerics had concentrated entirely on spiritual writings there would be far less literature remaining from pre-Conquest England. But this is a theme for later in the book and the question will be posed again in the proper place. Equally we might modify it and ask what relevance Old English literature has for the second half of the 20th century. The short answer to this question is that it is worth reading for its own sake, and our intention in this book is to demonstrate that this is so, and while doing so to provide a way of approaching this literature.

But because all art is a product of a particular mind in a particular place at a particular moment in time, we will begin by briefly describing the society in which these works which we now call collectively 'Old English literature' came to be written. It is possible to describe literature of other ages and other cultures (and, of course, works of art in general—but we will concentrate on literature from now on) in terms of the effect it has on me, the 20th-century reader with my 20th-century sensibility and knowledge, as I read it today. It is a valid approach, and one that has many adherents. On the other hand, a deeper, and one hopes more satisfying, interpretation can be derived from trying first to understand what the author was trying to do, and, more importantly, why he was trying to do it; this entails a historical approach and the imaginative reconstruction of the contemporary climate of thought.

The simplicity and directness of the *Lyrical Ballads* have their own immediate attractions, but an acquaintance with the mannered poetry of the Augustans which preceded them, and with the subsequent course of the Romantic Movement, of which these poems form a part, enables us to see what Wordsworth and Coleridge were trying to do, and how far they succeeded. There is a danger in this approach, and this is to overvalue the history and to neglect the literature; to place too much emphasis on the relationship between literature and its environment, and therefore to treat works of literature as social documents and to value them only for what they can tell us about the society in which they were produced. This temptation becomes the stronger as the amount of historical investigation needed increases and as the number of other sources decreases. It is fairly clear that 'The Leechgatherer' or the novels of Dickens do not have the same value for the historian as the reports of a Royal Commission or of an Edwin Chadwick. It is also clear that in default of this sort of source for the 8th century one may perhaps be able to use *Beowulf* to throw light on society; but it still remains a poem not a social document, and to esteem it only for what it can tell us about life before the Conquest would be utterly mistaken.

In linguistic studies there is a parallel division of approach between those who describe a language at a particular moment, who as it were take a snapshot of the language at one stage in its development (the synchronic approach), and those who follow the development of individual features of the language, like a time-lapse film of a growing plant (the diachronic approach). Here the dangers of each approach are clearer: that the synchronists may misinterpret features because they are not fully aware of their history: that the diachronists may be so involved in the history of separate features that they are unable to give a coherent account of the state of the language at any one time.

If we may declare our position here—and we had better, for to do otherwise would be sailing under false colours—we are firmly committed to the historical approach. C. S. Lewis several times used the simile of foreign travel, and distinguished between those who go abroad to learn foreign customs and the 'flavour' of the country, and those who take their Englishness abroad with them, protected from the foreignness of abroad by the anonymity of the standard tourist hotel. Now there is an air of superiority or cultural snobbishness about this simile, which we would not like to invoke; yet the fact remains that our preference would be for the first form of foreign travel even though it demands more effort from the traveller. But we should not forget, to return to literature, that this historical approach by way of the study of the background is only of use in so far as it leads us back to the literature with a greater understanding than before. If we do not appreciate the literature the more for having studied its setting, then as far as the literature goes we have been wasting our time.

ON CONTINUITY

It is an exaggeration, though not perhaps a very large one, to say that popular English history begins in 1066 with the Norman Conquest. This is reinforced by talk of ancestors coming over with the Conqueror and the like, as if the Normans kindly arrived to give the benefits of civilisation to the natives who couldn't even cook cakes without burning them (the most notorious incident in Anglo-Saxon history!). On the contrary, as we shall show, the decisive invasion in English history came six centuries earlier. The foundations of English society as we know it were laid not by the Normans but by the earlier Germanic invaders, the Angles, Saxons and others and their descendants, who by the time of the Conquest had formed a united nation with a consciousness of being English; who provided teachers and missionaries for Europe, even to the court of Charlemagne; whose art was famous; whose national tongue, English, had a flourishing vernacular literature.

When we compare old and new it is often the changes which stand out more than the similarities, and yet these similarities are no less important. A dog in an 18th-century portrait looks like no modern dog; the Tudor rose, still in cultivation, is quite different from this year's new roses. And yet there are still certain fundamental qualities common to the old and the new which enable us to say with confidence that they both are roses or both are dogs. Much of the comment on English is on the changes, on such matters as the shift of stress in such words as *dispute* or *controversy*, or the introduction of new, and therefore to some, unnecessary and ugly, words to describe new inventions or ideas, or on the acceptability of forms like *ain't* or *It's me*. Many books have been written on the changes in English, particularly on the growth of the vocabulary by borrowings from other languages. And indeed English, without the conservative influence of a body like the French Academy, has always been receptive of change. But important as these changes are, it still remains that English began as one of the Germanic family of languages, and still has at its heart a core of Germanic words, accounting for somewhere around two-thirds of present-day English. The proportion will vary according to the context: the country diary in a newspaper will contain a higher proportion of the Germanic than the first leader written often at a more abstract level. We would certainly be in difficulties if all foreign importations were proscribed from our language: we would hardly be able to speak at all if it was the native element that had been banned, for it forms the backbone of the language, and if the actual number of words is low in proportion to the importations yet the native words are the common ones and thus form a high proportion of the occurrences in any particular passage.

One of the phrases that Matthew Arnold used as a touchstone for the detection of the presence of the greatest poetry comes from *Hamlet*: 'Absent thee from felicity awhile.' Actually only two of these five words are from the Latin, but they do give the phrase its musical cadence that has an even stronger effect when set in its full context of the plain almost monosyllabic native:

> If thou didst ever hold me in thy heart,
> Absent thee from felicity awhile,
> And in this harsh world draw thy breath in pain,
> To tell my story.

V. ii

It is however a plainness that in the right place can have a power of its own even today. We don't need the latinate words to gain a rhetorical effect, though it is easier to talk in abstractions and to gloss over the situation in Latin-derived polysyllables:

> It cannot in the opinion of His Majesty's Government be classified as slavery in the extreme acceptance of the word without some risk of terminological inexactitude.   HANSARD 22 Feb. 1906, c. 555

Thus the Under Secretary of State for the Colonies trying to justify the Government's policy. Against it let us set another passage by the same speaker:

> Even though large tracts of Europe and many old and famous States have fallen or may fall into the grip of the Gestapo and all the odious apparatus of Nazi rule, we shall not flag or fail. We shall go on to the end. We shall fight in France, we shall fight on the seas and oceans, we shall fight with growing confidence and growing strength in the air, we shall defend our island, whatever the cost may be. We shall fight on the beaches, we shall fight on the landing grounds, we shall fight in the fields and in the streets, we shall fight in the hills; we shall never surrender.   HANSARD 4 June 1940, c. 796

Both are taken from Commons speeches by Winston Churchill at different stages in his career, but there is little doubt which is the more inspiring. Vocabulary apart, the second passage, which was delivered immediately after the fall of Dunkirk, owes much to the English tradition; it moves briskly and directly in short clauses of equal value, not in the multiplicity of subordinate clauses of the sentences of those who took the Latin period as their model. Compare this sentence taken almost at random from Johnson:

> Whether this opinion, so long transmitted and so widely propagated, had its beginning from truth and nature, or from accident and prejudice, whether it be decreed by the authority of reason, or the tyranny of ignorance, that of all the candidates for literary praise, the unhappy lexicographer holds the lowest place, neither vanity nor interest incited me to enquire.   THE PLAN OF A DICTIONARY 2

The Churchill passage follows the natural rhythm of speech, albeit of a higher style than everyday talk, but then nobody talks in periods like the one from Johnson; we have only to set against it a passage from an Old English sermon to show which the Churchill is more like. (The translation attempts to follow the sentence structure of the original.)

> And it came to pass as he said through learned men breaking their [monastic] rule, through laity breaking the law, through rich men's robberies, through the covetousness of ill-gotten gains, through lawlessness in the land, and through unjust [legal] decisions, through the sloth and folly of bishops, and through the wicked cowardice of God's messengers who kept silent about the truth all too often and mumbled with their mouths when they should have shouted.
>
> Wulfstan ADDRESS TO THE ENGLISH

So too with Old English verse; its patterns are selected from those of the natural speech rhythm of the language. As we shall see, it is stress-dependent, and the stresses still fall very much as they do today despite the changes in the language.

Here then is a second, longer, answer to our opening question. We believe Old English literature to be worth reading not only for its own sake because it is literature, but also because it is English as well as being Old, and that by knowing it our reading of other periods will be enriched, just as our reading of it is enriched by knowledge of what is to come.

A NOTE ON TRANSLATION

There are of course practical problems. Despite the continuity, English has changed in the last thousand years in other ways apart from the addition of new vocabulary. One cannot just pick up *Beowulf* and read it with no further ado; Chaucer, halfway nearer to us, still requires care, and we are shielded from Elizabethan English by modernised and normalised editions of Shakespeare. We have therefore used translations in this book, imperfect as they are, in an attempt to give something of the spirit of the literature. We cannot help feeling, however, that translations are very much a second best, particularly for poetry where we can convey the sense of the passage but less easily the tension between form and language that helps to make it poetry, and even if we could reproduce it there is a danger that the result would be a new poem entirely. Prose is perhaps less difficult. Old English prose was in the main utilitarian, and in its movement akin to modern English. Nevertheless the ideal would be for our readers to learn enough Old English to be able to read the originals, and for us to give the Old English. We have spared you this, but it is not too tall an order, firstly because it is easier to learn to read a language than to speak it, and secondly because it is not a foreign language, but an early form of English, disguised to some extent by accidentals of spelling and by strange letters in the alphabet. Whether it is worth the effort is a more personal question, but we have made it and our answer is this book.

2

Historical Background

From Caesar's first reconnaissance in 55 BC to the end of Roman rule in these islands is close on five hundred years, and for all except the first century lowland Britain was a province of the Roman Empire. Yet if we look around us, the influence of the Romans on the way we live now is almost non-existent, apart from a scattering of archaeological sites, the names and positions of some of our cities, and the line of some of our roads, which in any case are influenced by natural features. The tantalising thing is that while a great deal is known about the course of the Roman invasion and occupation and of life in Roman Britain, we know next to nothing of what happened in the two centuries after the legions left; yet these two centuries were far more important than the preceding five, for in them were laid the foundations of England.

In the 3rd and 4th centuries AD there came increasing pressure from the east on the Roman Empire, which then stretched from the Sahara to the Clyde and from Gibraltar to Asia Minor and the shores of the Caspian. This pressure was nothing new. From prehistoric times the movement of peoples in Europe and Western Asia has been westward. Successive migrations have come one after the other like ripples on a pond. The Greeks, the Romans themselves, and the Celts all had their origins farther east. Now the next wave had come, and the Germanic peoples were pushing westward and breaching the frontiers of the Empire. In AD 410 the Goths under Alaric sacked Rome itself: in 455 the Vandals had their turn, and their fame lives on in the modern connotations of their name. The consequence was that Britain, like other fringes of the Empire, could be held no longer. In 410 the last of the Roman legions left Britain to help meet Alaric's threats on Rome, and though there seems to have been a brief reoccupation it can have been neither extensive nor long lived.

The details of what happened next are far from clear. This period is the most obscure of all our history. By the middle of the 5th century the raids by Germanic tribes from across the North Sea, which had started well before the Romans left, had become first invasions, then settlements. Gradually, though not without setbacks, one of which can be attributed to the historical Arthur, the invaders pushed north and west, driving the British from the richer farm lands of the south and east to the less desirable uplands of the 'Celtic fringe'. The mists do not begin to clear again until the end of the next century, when Christianity, and with it writing, was once more brought to these shores. Meanwhile in the two intervening centuries the foundations of England were laid, in the last invasion in which the invaders were in sufficient strength to impose their patterns permanently on the country.

One thing at any rate is certain; that the invaders were from the Germanic tribes. According to Bede, they came from the three most formidable peoples of Germany, the Saxons, Angles and Jutes. Procopius, an earlier historian from Byzantium, calls them Angles and Frisians. Whatever their exact origins—Bede's division into three may well reflect an attempt to make a coherent pattern out of an untidy and confused situation—there is no doubt that they were all Germans. The language of their descendants two or three centuries later belongs to the western branch of the Germanic family, and in fact shares with Frisian the sound changes which separate it from German and Dutch. Archaeology and place-name studies, too, confirm that they came from the coastal areas stretching from the mouth of the Rhine up to southern Denmark.

By the beginning of the 7th century there were a dozen independent kingdoms in England. The two north of the Humber were united at about this time into the Kingdom of Northumbria. The ten or so south of the Humber likewise gradually diminished in number as the smaller and weaker units acknowledged the overlordship of their more powerful neighbours. Eventually two major kingdoms were left: Mercia in the midlands and Wessex south of the Thames. The important thing to note is the difference between north and south. Again and again the Humber is felt to be a significant boundary dividing those living to the north of it from the southern English. This distinction (which incidentally can be seen on a modern map in that the counties south of the Humber which are pre-Conquest in origin are generally much smaller than the six northern counties) comes less from a difference in the original settlers than from the isolation in the early period caused by the continued existence of the Celtic Kingdom of Elmet in southern Yorkshire between the Pennines and the Humber astride the lines of communication, and in later times by the existence of a Norse kingdom at York.

The pattern of relationships between the kingdoms was changing all the time. From the 7th century onwards there was usually one king strong enough for his authority to be recognised throughout the country. But his wider authority was purely a personal matter which did not automatically pass to his successor. In the 7th century from the reign of Edwin, which saw the fall of Elmet, the king of Northumbria had this authority; in the next century it passed south to Mercia under Æthelbald and Offa; in the early 9th century Egbert of Wessex came nearest yet to becoming king of all England.

However, this gradual progress towards national unity was disturbed from outside. The first signs were the Viking attacks on three of the most important centres of the Church in northern Britain in three successive years: Lindisfarne in 793, Jarrow in 794 and Iona in 795; but it was not for another forty years that the raids became really serious. The Vikings, finding the country unprepared and a fruitful source of plunder, came across the North Sea from Scandinavia in the spring and returned in the autumn after a summer of profitable raiding.

Eventually they turned from raiding to settlement. Perhaps the supply of plunder was drying up; perhaps their growing acquaintance with the country suggested another way of exploiting it. In 865 the Danes invaded in force. Their Great Army spent the next ten years moving up and down the country, and was overrunning Wessex in 870–871 when Alfred succeeded his brother. He managed to keep them at bay, and they did not return till 876–878 after their thoughts had turned to permanent settlement. Reduced at one point to the Athelney marshes in Somerset, Alfred fought back, winning a decisive victory over the Danes in the early summer of 878 near Chippenham. Their leader Guthrum received baptism and led his force away to East Anglia, which he settled in 879. The Danish settlements were largely in the east. In the north and west, Norse Vikings, whose route led round Scotland to Ireland by way of Orkney, Shetland and the Western Isles, made settlements in Cheshire, the Wirral and up the Lancashire and Cumberland coasts, and also penetrated through the Aire gap to York. As a result, much of northern and eastern England south of the Tees and east of Watling Street, the modern A5, was heavily settled and ruled by Scandinavians.

Wessex, therefore, was the only one of the old kingdoms to escape relatively unscathed. The remainder of Alfred's reign was devoted to repairing the damage done by the invaders rather than in trying to drive them out. After his death in 899 his son and grandson gradually brought the Danish areas under their control while allowing them a certain degree of autonomy, and a new period of prosperity and cultural revival began, in which West Saxon became the standard English. But peace was not to last. From 980 onwards came a fresh round of Danish invasions in search of tribute rather than plunder which lasted through the reign of Æthelred the Unready and culminated in a Danish king, Cnut (Canute), becoming the first king of all England in 1016.

Fifty years later came the Normans. William was careful to stress the legality of his claim to the throne, and began by trying to preserve as much continuity as possible with the reign of Edward, whose death had precipitated the crisis. Nevertheless the Norman Conquest marks the end of the Anglo-Saxon period, and the beginning of the end of Old English. The Normans were originally Scandinavians who had settled in France at about the same time as the Danes had settled in England, and they had quickly assimilated themselves to their new home. After the revolt of 1069 had shown that William's policy of retaining the English administration had failed, the new leaders of Church and State were French speaking, and furthermore were in general men of action rather than men of culture. As a result English—the standard English of Wessex—was no longer employed either in the processes of government or in the entertainment of the governing classes. Furthermore the English skill in the arts was no longer in demand and fell away. The language, of course, survived, and after an interval again became the language of government and of culture, but its external form had developed; Old English had become Middle English, the language of Chaucer, and hence beyond our present scope.

THE IMPACT OF CHRISTIANITY

Of all the external influences on the English, the coming of Christianity is without a doubt the most important. Differences in moral outlook apart, the conversion of England meant that she was brought into regular contact with a wider, more cosmopolitan world, and back into the mainstream of European civilisation; it meant that there was a need for education and for books to keep the routine of the Church alive; it provided a new set of images for poets and artists.

In the closing years of the 1st century AD, Tacitus, the Roman historian and civil servant, wrote a report on the origin and geography of Germany for the guidance of the Emperor Trajan who was then engaged in a military campaign against the German tribes across the Rhine from the Roman province of Gaul. Part of his purpose is propaganda for home consumption; he points the contrast between the growing softness of Rome and the keen warlike spirit of the Germans. But on the whole his account has been shown to be reliable, and it remains one of the best pieces of independent evidence of how the German tribes lived in their continental home. When he comes to the way of life of the German warriors his story is borne out not only by later literature but also by the lives of historical persons even centuries later. He explains that all business is transacted in arms, and that the award of arms by a chief or elder kinsman marks a boy's coming of age. He will then join a chief's band of companions.

They join the rest of the older men who have long proved themselves, and it is no shame to be seen in a band of companions. There are various ranks in a band assigned by the judgment of the chief. And so there is great rivalry among the companions for the foremost place by the chief's side, and amongst chiefs for the most numerous and keenest companions. This is the source of their position and power: continual attendance by a body of chosen youths brings respect in peace and protection in war. If a chief becomes noted for the number and courage of his band of companions, his fame and reputation is not confined to his own tribe but spreads to adjoining ones as well. Chiefs are courted by embassies, and rewarded with gifts and often bring wars to an end by their reputation alone.

When it comes to battle, it is a disgrace for a chief to be surpassed in valour; for his followers not to match up to the valour of their chief. Furthermore it is lifelong infamy and disgrace to have left the battle alive after the death of the chief. To defend and protect him, to ascribe to his credit one's own brave deeds is the essence of their sworn allegiance. The chiefs fight for victory; the companions for their chief. If the land of their birth is stagnating in a lengthy period of peace and quiet, many noble youths on their own account seek out other tribes which are at war, because peace is not welcome to this people; they can win renown more easily amidst perils, nor can a large band of companions be maintained but by violence and war. Companions are always making demands on the generosity of their chief for 'that much-prized war-horse' or 'that blood-stained and victorious spear'. But meals and feasts with their plain but plentiful fare are just counted as pay. The means of providing all this is war and plunder. You will not persuade a German to plough the land and wait for the yearly crops as easily as you will to challenge an enemy and earn the prize of wounds. . . .

The chiefs take special delight in gifts from neighbouring tribes, which are sent not only by private individuals but also by the people as a whole—choice horses, magnificent arms, metal discs and collars, and we have even taught them to value money.

Tacitus GERMANIA xiii–xv

This relationship between a chief and his companions goes far to explain much of early English history. The need for a continual income is the main motive behind the Viking raids; nor is it purely coincidence that the kingdoms which grew most in power were Northumbria, Mercia and Wessex, all of which bordered unconquered territory from which retainers might be rewarded.

Again, leadership amongst the Germans was a personal matter. Here is one reason for the fluctuation of the pattern of relationships between the kingdoms up to the period of the Danish invasions. King Edwin of Northumbria (d. 632) was the first to win the allegiance of all the other kings apart from Kent. But it was an allegiance of individuals, much the same as that of chief and companions. Edwin stood at the transition between the old paganism and Christianity. He accepted the new religion, but converted Northumbria relapsed after his death. His life, too, has much of the old heroic outlook about it. He had spent his youth away from home, partly among the British, but later as an exile with King Rædwald of East Anglia, then overlord of the kingdoms south of the Humber; here he had known what it is for one's life to depend upon a conflict between a host's honour and his desire for gain. He returned to his father's kingdom with the aid of his protector Rædwald, and made himself in turn lord of other kings, and his own retainers were prepared to die for him. Bede tells of one, Lilla, who lost his life when he interposed his own body between Edwin and an assassin's thrust, there being no other protection available. Edwin's own death came in battle on the borders of his kingdom, as one of his sons fell with him while the others were hustled to safety by a faithful retainer.

Britain had been Christian long before the English settlement, but the native Christians had little influence on the pagan invaders who had diminished their contact with the Roman mother church. Thus the Celtic church went its own way, and developed its own distinctive forms of piety and discipline. The most obvious difference between them was the method of calculating the date of Easter, which is a complex problem involving the reconciliation of the lunar and the solar year. Though fierce controversy raged over this issue, the more fundamental differences were in outlook and organisation. The Celtic church combined an ascetic monasticism with missionary zeal and a love of seclusion. (Even the first Norse settlers in Iceland found Irish hermits already there before them.) Its organisation, however, was more suited to winning converts than to the subsequent administration of the church. Bishops were not given control of a fixed diocese, but instead were free to go and preach and work where the need was greatest, while the control of the church in an area fell to the abbot of the chief monastery.

The Celtic church had much influence particularly in the north, and gave much, especially of her scholarship and art, but in the end the authority of Rome won the day. The first mission from Rome, sent by Pope Gregory, arrived in Kent in 597 under the leadership of an Italian monk, Augustine. The difference between the Celtic and Roman churches was settled at the Synod of Whitby in 664 in Rome's favour, thus ensuring that the new English church would follow Rome. But it took about a century for the old paganism to die out and for the new religion to become secure. The transition was eased by a policy of adaptation; even now Easter takes its name from the pagan goddess whose feast was celebrated in the spring. Similarly, pagan temples often were not destroyed but reconsecrated as churches; Rædwald of East Anglia is even said to have had a pagan and a Christian altar side by side in the same building—an example of hedging one's bets if there ever was one.

The coming of the Church meant a need for native priests, and the need for priests meant a need for formal education in reading, writing, Latin and music so that the liturgy of the Church could be followed properly. Even before Gregory had sent Augustine on his mission, he had directed that some of the revenues of the Church in Gaul should be applied to the purchase of young English slaves who were to be placed in monasteries for training. Of the earliest schools we know nothing except that they must have existed in the early centres of Christianity; the more notable ones came later. Of these the ones at Canterbury and York were the equal of any in Europe. The school at Canterbury was refounded by a Greek, Theodore of Tarsus, and a North African, Hadrian. They were sent from Rome and arrived in 669 when the English church was at a low ebb after a severe outbreak of plague. The school quickly became established as a noted centre of scholarship, where even Greek was taught. The school at York was founded in the 8th century by Archbishop Egbert, a pupil of Bede. Its fame, however, was greatest under Alcuin from 767 to 782, when it attracted pupils from the continent. In fact Alcuin's fame was such that when he met Charlemagne on a journey to Rome he was invited to the Frankish court, where from 782 onwards he was head of the palace school, contributing English scholarship to the revival of learning under Charlemagne.

Education of course needs books, and the provision of libraries was seen to be an important part of the founding of monasteries. How important can be shown from the use made of them. In 669 Theodore and Hadrian were accompanied from Rome by Benedict Biscop, a Northumbrian nobleman turned monk, who was on his first visit. He spent some years at Canterbury with them as abbot of the nearby monastery of St. Peter and St. Paul. He later made three more journeys to Rome to collect books and relics for the monasteries which he founded at Monkwearmouth and Jarrow, and he gave instructions that these libraries should not be dispersed on his death. His successor, Ceolfrith, added to them, to make them even more splendid. They were not, of course, unique, but the importance of these particular ones is the greater when we remember that Bede spent most of his life at Jarrow, working with these books. Since he wrote in Latin, his output does not immediately concern us; but he was a major scholar of international standing whose works include a long series of commentaries on the Bible, scientific works, particularly on chronology, and, most famous today, his *History of the English Church*. Without the resources of a good library he could have achieved none of this. But the traffic in books was not one way only. English monasteries had their scriptoria where manuscripts were copied, and their products made their way back to the continent. One example must suffice. In the early 8th century

Ceolfrith ordered three copies to be made of the text of the Vulgate which Benedict had brought from Rome. Two of these were intended for Monkwearmouth and Jarrow, but apart from a few fragments in the British Museum and at Durham they have now perished; Ceolfrith set out with the third in 716 as a gift for the Pope. He died on the journey but the Bible survived, and is known today as the *Codex Amiatinus* from the name of the convent at Monte Amiato near Siena where it was rediscovered in modern times.

THE ANGLO-SAXON ACHIEVEMENT

Apart from literature, probably the most enduring of the arts is architecture; it is certainly the most conspicuous. In a way this is unfortunate, for architecture is one of the weak points of Anglo-Saxon culture. On their first arrival in this country the English were among the least civilised of the German tribes. They were not town dwellers, and had no use for the Roman buildings with their central heating and plumbing. In fact they seem to have stood in awe of them if the references to ruins in their poetry are anything to go by. Their natural building material was timber, not brick or stone, and timber is perishable and offers less scope to the builder. The Church authorities, however, used stone for churches and followed Roman traditions of church architecture, but even so they had to import masons. Benedict Biscop brought men from France when he was building his monasteries at Jarrow and Monkwearmouth. There were other great builders: Wilfrid built churches at Hexham, Ripon and York, but of these buildings only the crypts at Hexham and Ripon survive because more splendid buildings were later erected on their sites. Thus evidence of Anglo-Saxon architecture is scanty by the nature of the case; but what there is suggests that the English preferred to spend their resources on other more showy objects: on decoration, jewellers' work, precious reliquaries, crosses and plate, rich vestments or splendid books, rather than on mere masonry. The Normans, on the other hand, were great builders; their obvious superiority in this field has tended to obscure English achievements in other areas of civilisation.

By the time of the Conquest, England was a united nation and felt herself to be one. In the reign of Edward the Confessor, trouble broke out between north and south, and civil war appeared to be imminent, but was averted at the last minute because 'it was hateful to them that they should fight against men of their own kin, because there were very few who were worth much in each army who were not Englishmen'. There was a standard 'King's English' known and used throughout the country, and mentioned in Icelandic saga. It was used not only for literature but also for administration. There was a well organised legal system—or two if one allows for the legal peculiarities of the Danelaw—and the earliest written code of law in any Germanic language is written in English.

When we turn to the arts the picture is even more remarkable, though we are handicapped by the scanty and piecemeal nature of what has survived. Yet the work of English craftsmen was famed throughout Europe as we know from literary sources. Even the monastery of Monte Cassino in Italy, the mother house of the Benedictine order, could find nothing more suitable to house its most precious relic, a fragment of the towel with which Christ dried His disciples' feet, than an English-made casket 'most subtly and beautifully decorated with gold and jewels in the English style'. And indeed Norman historians express amazement at the riches to be found in England, a land which 'surpasses France many times over in abundance of precious metal', for English women 'have great skill with the needle and golden embroidery, and the men in every craft', thus attracting 'Germans with the most knowledge of these arts' and also merchants from far and wide. Little enough has survived, particularly of textiles, but the stole from the tomb of St. Cuthbert, which is still at Durham in the Cathedral Library, embroidered at the orders of Queen Ælfflæd between 909 and 916, is some measure of how great our loss is.

Most of the art that has survived is ecclesiastical—another witness to the importance of the Church. In part this is because the Church was far the largest patron of the arts in her own right, and also the recipient of gifts from laymen wishing to gain merit by adding to the splendour of the Church and her services. And this remained true until the Reformation. In part, again, churches are places where treasures have a better chance of survival. Fire and thieves respect no man, but a church does provide continuity of ownership and a resting place for such as escape those ravagers.

Nevertheless we are not without examples of pagan art; in fact one collection of treasure from this period is as rich as anything in Europe, and without equal in this country. This is the Sutton Hoo treasure, which has survived to our day because it was placed in the cenotaph of an East Anglian king in the middle of the 7th century, somewhere around 650–660. It was excavated in 1939 and is now on display in the British Museum. The largest burial mound in an Anglo-Saxon cemetery near the coast of East Anglia not far from Ipswich was found to have contained a ship 80 or 90 feet long (the timbers had decayed entirely and the ends of the ship were gone but its outline could still be traced in the sandy soil), and in it was what was obviously a royal treasure but no trace of any human remains. There were a standard and a whetstone sceptre, weapons and armour, jewellery, continental coins, domestic utensils, and the fragments of a stringed instrument. Not all is English by any means: there is a large Coptic silver bowl from Alexandria, and other silver from the East and from the Celtic West; the helmet from the set of armour looks Swedish in style. Here then is tangible proof of the extent of European trade in the Dark Ages. But what is more staggering is the richness of it all. East Anglia was by no means one of the most powerful kingdoms, nor would those who buried this treasure in honour of their dead king have emptied the royal treasury; the living need riches too. England is an island, but then it was not insular any more than it is now, and the standard of living of this royal household must have been the equal of any in Europe. On this evidence England must have been rich indeed before the Vikings came.

The second great influence on English culture was the Celtic world. Its actual effect on art we must pass over, for it is better described in pictures not words, except to point out that the intermingling of traditions in Northumbria in the 7th and 8th centuries, where the Celtic church was strongest, produced a school of illumination whose products are found all over Europe as well as in Dublin itself. But Celtic scholarship and missionary zeal are important also. The influence of Celtic scholarship shows itself more particularly in Latin writings where there is a tendency to an extremely convoluted prose style. As for missionary zeal, twice before the Conquest the English were the schoolmasters of Europe. The first occasion came when, even before the conversion of England was complete, English missionaries went to work in the Low Countries and the Rhineland, which is no doubt why there are statues of British saints on the bridge over the Main at Würzburg. The first men were Northumbrians, most of them with Irish experience or training. They were later joined by the West Saxon, Boniface, whose name is most closely associated with this mission. Their work included reforming the Frankish church and bringing it back into contact with Rome and the mainstream of European life, as well as missionary work among the unconverted nations, and made possible the renaissance under Charlemagne a generation later, at the centre of which was another Englishman, Alcuin of York.

The second occasion came two centuries later, when in the monastic revival of the 10th century the English church played a large but unquantifiable part in the conversion of Scandinavia, in particular Sweden and Norway, and with Norway Iceland. The earlier missionaries to Germany carried on an extensive correspondence with friends and advisers back in England, and much of it has survived. There is nothing similar for the Scandinavian missions. We have only isolated references to the work of English bishops and priests; with Hakon the Good in Norway, for example, or going there with Olaf Tryggvason in 995; to a bishop working in Norway in the reign of Sweyn Forkbeard, and so on. But the evidence for a considerable English influence is there in such matters as the rituals of the Norwegian church, or in the design of some of its buildings, or even in the script of Icelandic manuscripts. The rest, however, is silence.

Our last witness to the civilisation of the Anglo-Saxons is their literature, but here we must reserve our defence to the following chapters, except to remark that though it has later rivals, that of Iceland for example, for its time no other vernacular literature in Europe can touch it.

Thus it was not to a nation of savages that the Normans came. In many ways their coming was a disaster for it brought a check to many aspects of English culture. It was not a sudden death but a decline within a generation or so, as artists and craftsmen alive at the Conquest found no successors. This decline is obvious in many fields where a chronological sequence can be set out for examination, be it of coins of the realm or illuminated manuscripts, but in no field is it as obvious as in literature, where Old English went on being written for almost a century but eventually disappeared, only to reappear in a new guise—an altered form of English, but nevertheless English once more.

3

Prose Writings

'Par ma foi! il y a plus de quarante ans que je dis de la prose sans que j'en susse rien.' 'Good heavens! I've been talking prose for over forty years without realising it.' Molière's Bourgeois Gentilhomme can speak for us all, for good prose is not obtrusive, whether it is spoken or written. In most languages prose writing developed as a medium for the preservation and transmission of useful information. Early prose is nearly always utilitarian; it records what people need to know and remember accurately. That this is as true of Old English prose can be shown by listing the kinds that have survived.

(1) *Legal*. The laws of Æthelberht of Kent are the earliest of the surviving codes of Anglo-Saxon law, and the earliest Old English prose. They date from the later part of his reign from some time after Augustine's landing in 597 to his own death in 616, for they are a product of a revision of the old Kentish laws to take account of the coming of Christianity and in particular of a church that owned property, while the Church herself brought the literate clergy who made the writing down of the code possible. Other major early codes are those of Hlothere and Eadric (685–6) and Wihtred (690–6) from Kent, and Ine (688–725) from Wessex. Later Alfred and Cnut both issued important codifications of the law of their day. Apart from codes of law, many other legal documents have survived, both wills, originally spoken verbally, and charters, more formal documents usually recording the disposition of land or other gifts. Today these works fall largely in the province of the student of history or language.

(2) *Religious*. This is by far the largest category, containing

sermons, saints' lives and translations of and commentaries on the Bible, and also a few books of instruction on the religious life, chief among which are King Alfred's translation of St. Gregory's *Pastoral Care* and a commentary on the Benedictine Rule.

(3) *Historical.* The chief item is the *Anglo-Saxon Chronicle* which is discussed more fully below. There are also translations of Latin originals, including the *Ecclesiastical History* of Bede, the first English historian to write scientific history as opposed to an uncritical acceptance of legend and folk-lore.

(4) *Medical.* Much of the Old English medical writings could be called folk-lore or old wives' tales. It consists of prescriptions and accounts of the medicinal properties of natural products, animal and vegetable. The most famous text is rather more than this, however. The *Leechbook of Bald* (Bald was an early owner) has 155 chapters each dealing with a different condition, and a collection of prescriptions which has no organic connection with the first part of the book. Another work, the *Peri Didaxeon* or *Schools of Medicine*, shows the extent of Continental contacts, for it contains translations of material from the celebrated medical school at Salerno, south of Naples; its prescriptions have none of the superstitious magic that marks the other collections.

(5) *Scientific.* The most considerable work is Byrhtferth's *Manual.* Byrhtferth was a monk from Ramsey in Huntingdonshire who wrote for the instruction of the parish clergy. He sets down in simple language the elements of astronomy and mathematics—the proper calculation of the date of Easter always loomed large in the early Church. Apart from this there are the elements of medicine and science in general, multiplication tables, weights and measures (his statement that there are 240 pence and 20 shillings in a pound remained good for 960 years), and grammar. As a handbook it is only rivalled by Ælfric's *De Temporibus Anni*, which as the title, *On the Seasons of the Year*, suggests is limited to chronology and astronomy.

(6) *Educational.* The intention of Byrhtferth's *Manual* was educational, but there were other books more specifically intended for use in the monastic schools. Ælfric, for example, translated the Latin grammar of Priscian, the standard textbook

of the time, and added a Latin-English glossary. His *Colloquium*, a dialogue in Latin on everyday subjects, was intended to teach the language painlessly by the direct method to novices in the monastery at Winchester. Of the two manuscripts, the one in the British Museum has an English crib written in between the lines.

These writings have many subjects but only one purpose, to inform or exhort. Entertainment came second, though there is no intrinsic reason why information should not be imparted entertainingly. We have, it is true, one fragment of a secular prose tale—*Apollonius of Tyre*, based on a lost Latin version of the original Greek, but it is only one fragment amongst a host of more utilitarian pieces. Why is this? To begin with the obvious, written prose cannot exist before writing, whereas poetry can be composed and remembered without being written down, since its versification is an aid to memory. Thus oral poetry is always earlier than written prose, and is used in the beginning also for subjects that are later seen to be more suitable for prose when once it becomes available and advancing literacy leads to a declining ability to memorise long passages. The transfer from poetry to prose begins with the most utilitarian, with things like laws where the necessary precision of wording may be difficult to achieve in verse. But writing in the Middle Ages was almost exclusively confined to the Church, which needed it for administration and for maintenance of the correct forms of the liturgy, and the language of the Church was Latin. Thus in the early part of the Old English period most prose is being written in Latin. (Æthelberht's laws are an exception; they are written in English presumably because of the difficulty in the early days of finding Latin equivalents for the terms of Germanic law.)

Writing is difficult and expensive; therefore one test of whether to commit something to writing is 'Is it useful?' Everything had to be written by hand; printing was not developed until the later 15th century. Materials were crude by our standards: quill pens and home-made ink. They were also expensive: paper is a post-Conquest arrival. Until it was brought to Europe from the East by the Arabs, the normal writing material was vellum or parchment, the prepared skins of farm animals. Thus writing was a serious business, not to be taken lightly, as we may jot down notes with a ball-point pen in a cheap notebook. A large manuscript needs the skins of a considerable number of animals. Just how serious a business can perhaps be seen from a 15th-century writer's defence of his craft. Thomas Hoccleve was a writer in the office of the Privy Seal at the beginning of the century who found it necessary to answer those who thought writing an easy job in comparison with manual labour. He points out the difficulty of concentrating the mind, eye and hand together, and the impossibility of talking at the same time, which makes the job seem longer:

> A writer mot thre thyngës to hym knytte,
> And in tho may be no disseuerance;
> Mynde, ee, and hand, non may fro othir flitte,
>   But in hem mot be ioynt continuance.
>   The mynde, al hoole with-outen variance,
>   On the ee and hand awaytë moot alway,
>   And thei two eek on hym; it is no nay.
>
> Who so schal wrytë, may nat holde a tale
> With hym and hym, ne syngë this ne that;
> But al his wittës hoolë, grete and smale,
>   Ther must appere, and halden hem ther-at;
>   And syn, he spekë may, ne syngë nat,
>   But bothë two he nedës moot forbere,
>   Hir labour to hym is the alengere.

DE REGIMINE PRINCIPUM 995–1008

Besides the practical difficulties there were moral ones. Writing was a clerical occupation, using 'clerical' in its original sense; those who could read and write were in holy orders, and most of the surviving manuscripts were written at monasteries, for writing as well as reading was part of the study prescribed by the Benedictine Rule. This imposes a set of priorities that we could wish to have been different. There are some things that must be written down for practical reasons. If when these have been written one still has time and material available to write with, then one should employ it for the greater glory of God and the salvation of souls. If we take this attitude into consideration we should be surprised that so much that is not strictly utilitarian has survived. The first obstacle to its survival is getting it written down in the first place; the second is the disposal of 'worthless' material in monastery libraries—we shall later come to fragments of poetry that were only preserved in the bindings of other volumes; the third is the dissolution of the monasteries when many a great library was despoiled, and by no means all their contents came safely into the hands of private collectors; nor were they safe even then. The collection made by Sir Robert Cotton, one of the most assiduous private collectors, now in the British Museum, suffered a disastrous fire in 1731 which destroyed some manuscripts and damaged more.

Thus the prose we have is largely prose of information and instruction, not entertainment. But prose does not need literary value to be good prose; it is good if it transmits clearly and unobtrusively what its author intended to convey. Here Old English prose scored several notable successes. But out of the categories mentioned above we are going to comment only on the plain instructional prose of King Alfred and the *Anglo-Saxon Chronicle*, and on the more emotional exhortatory prose of Ælfric and Wulfstan; amongst these four can be found the best Old English prose.

ALFRED

On the whole, English royalty has not been noted for devotion to the arts. So Alfred's combination of military prowess with scholarship may seem at first to be a little incongruous. It is certainly remarkable for a layman to have done so much in an age when the clergy were the chief authors, scribes and teachers. Yet his literary work is all of a piece with his military; in both he was seeking the welfare of his people. The campaigns of the early years of his reign brought an uneasy settlement with the Danes, and gave a precarious peace, twice broken, in which the work of reconstruction of his ravaged kingdom could proceed. Naturally his first concern was for the necessities of everyday life and their protection. He greatly increased the preparedness and fighting power of Wessex by building fortresses and ships and by reorganising the militia to make it a more efficient fighting force, and these preparations stood him in good stead in his later campaigns. But, bodily needs apart, he was also concerned for the spiritual welfare of his people.

Born in 849 at Wantage in Berkshire he had been to Rome twice while he was still very young, which is more than most of us can say for ourselves in this age of mass travel. But whereas we mostly go as tourists to see the sights, he went as a pilgrim to the hub of the civilised world, and was received by the Pope, the head of the Church in the West. Altogether it must have been an enormous stimulus to an alert and enquiring mind. He grew up in a cultured and devout family. His father, King Æthelwulf, was a religious man who took more interest in his private devotions than in encounters with the Danes. His mother encouraged her children to appreciate the Germanic legends of their ancestors, and often recited English poetry to them. But despite any early interests—he could read English by the time he was twelve, and this in an age when literacy was confined to the clergy—the harsh realities of life could not be put aside. From the time he was old enough to bear weapons until he was nearly thirty he was engaged in fighting the Danish invaders with little respite, until in 878 he stood godfather to their leader Guthrum when he accepted baptism after the Battle of Edington.

In the interval between the wars of 886 and 892 Alfred began to turn to the other part of his mission, the education and spiritual welfare of his people. Like Charlemagne before him, he began by searching out teachers to help restore the learning that had been lost. He found men from Mercia, from the Celtic lands and from the Continent, and with their help learnt to read and translate Latin. Fruition came in translation of five books which he produced or presided over between 894 and his death in 899. These translations, the foundations of English prose literature, are part of an educational programme to restore the old state of learning in England when kings feared God and clergy were zealous for learning, teaching and the service of God, and when people flocked from abroad to English teachers.

Preoccupation with war had taken men's minds from learning and there were few left who could understand Latin. Monasteries were no longer havens of peace since their treasures had become the targets of Viking attack. In Bede and Alcuin England had had scholars of international repute, but they had had no successors to come anywhere near them, and when Alfred's first translation appeared Alcuin had been dead for 90 years and Bede for a century and a half.

This first translation was the *Pastoral Care* of Gregory, the pope who had sent Augustine on his mission to England in 596. In it Gregory, by outlining the heavy responsibilities of a bishop, sought to excuse his own reluctance to assume the papal throne. In the early Church there was less of a distinction than there now is between the roles of priest and bishop, and Gregory's work was widely used as a model for the instruction of parish clergy, and this together with the stress on the bishop's duty to instruct the laity account for its primacy among Alfred's translations. The next two were Bede's *History of the English Church*—the translation which appears least likely to be by Alfred himself from the style and from the dialect which has Mercian features—and a history of the ancient world, the *History against the Pagans* by Orosius, a 5th-century Spanish disciple of St. Augustine of Hippo. These two books together give an account of the origin and traditions of Christianity in England and of the history and geography of the known world, for to Orosius's account of the Mediterranean lands Alfred added all that he had been able to find out about Central and Northern Europe. His last two translations move from the physical world to the realm of ideas. The author of the first of these, Boethius (d. AD 524), stands at the meeting point between Classical antiquity and Christian Europe. He came from a Roman family which had given distinguished public service in the past, and he followed in this tradition, but fell from favour under Theodoric the Goth, and was imprisoned and put to death. In his last months he wrote in prison his *De Consolatione Philosophiae*, a final personal statement of the value of philosophy, and one of the seminal books of the Middle Ages. In it Alfred found a firm belief that man should, by exercising his will, rise above his fate by accepting it, for whatever disasters may befall are irrelevant to the man who can follow out the workings of divine providence. Alfred's last book, though he called it an anthology, is closely based on the first book of St. Augustine's *Soliloquies*, in which the theme is immortality and how the soul may come to know God.

Exciting is not really the right word for Alfred's translations. They are workmanlike attempts to use the language to express more than a bare recital of facts, and when he was writing, English was an untried medium at this level. As he says himself, he sometimes translates word for word and sometimes paraphrases. He is governed by his originals but not so slavishly that he cannot break away from the Latin periodic sentence (which despite its later skilful employment by Dr. Johnson sits unnaturally in English), or add his own comments and glosses to the text he is translating. The most extended of these are the passages he added to Orosius, in which he retells the voyages of the Norwegian Ohthere along the outer coast of Scandinavia round past the North Cape to the White Sea, and of another traveller, Wulfstan, in Baltic waters from Slesvig to the mouth of the Vistula. Both these travels reappear in Hakluyt's *Voyages*, and there are those who say Alfred's version is finer than the Elizabethan. But perhaps more typical are the shorter interjections and illustrations from daily life which he uses to explain and expand on his texts. In fact many will find that it is the passages where he is speaking with his own voice that are the ones which most come to life. In this he is rather like Malory six centuries later. Malory, too, is extending the range of English prose at the very beginning of modern English by working from foreign sources to produce his Arthurian romance. But his *Morte d'Arthur* is less of a translation and more of an original work. Even so the strain of working in an untried medium shows from time to time, and the passages where he turns to the reader in his own voice can clearly be seen to be less constrained. The same is true of Alfred; the difference for us is that we find Malory's subject-matter intrinsically more interesting. What is exciting about Alfred is that he was tackling the problems of vernacular prose writing so early; what is sad is that the course of history undid his work.

The Anglo-Saxon Chronicle, if not actually a product of Alfred's educational programme, was compiled in his reign and most likely in the period when the translations were being made. The early part (it begins with Caesar's invasion of Britain in 54 BC) must come from secondary sources and is thus of less interest, but from 449 onwards it draws upon early traditions in its annalistic account of the coming of the English and their subsequent history, becoming fuller in its treatment of events as it approaches the date of compilation and can use living memory. Such a history would certainly fit in with Alfred's programme of education, and help to strengthen feelings of nationhood in his subjects. Copies were made and distributed to important centres, where some were continued. Seven manuscripts survive, but their relationships with these copies and with each other is a complicated and confused question. One called the *Parker Chronicle* because it once belonged to Matthew Parker the Elizabethan archbishop and collector, came originally from Winchester. It was written around 900—from the beginning to 891 it is in one hand—and was continued in a variety of contemporary hands until 1070. Another, the *Peterborough Chronicle*, is written in one hand up to 1121 from a text originating at Canterbury and was continued at Peterborough until 1154, the last of the Chronicles to be kept up. The dates and coverage of the other five manuscripts fall between these two.

The *Chronicle* has been compared to a diary with entries for years instead of days, and the analogy has a lot of truth in it, for it is not a connected, coherent history, though in places the story does run on from year to year. It is patchy like a diary; there are many years without an entry, and many entries are obviously written up later to fill gaps. Some entries are so brief as to give almost a surrealist view of events, just as the notes in an old diary often show that the preoccupations of the moment are not always with what is going to have long-term importance.

But it says what it has to say plainly and not without a touch of poetic imagination even in the baldest entries such as this one:

473 Here [*i.e.* In this year] Hengest and Æsch fought with the Welsh and took untold plunder, and the Welsh fled the English like fire.

This is a simple entry that can be translated word for word without even altering the order of the words. But more complicated later narratives are told in a similar plain style. The entry for 1048 tells of a disturbance at Dover when Count Eustace of Boulogne and his men provoked a riot. Eustace then gave a false account to his brother-in-law, King Edward, which led eventually to the outlawry of Earl Godwine and his sons:

And then Eustace came from across the sea shortly after the bishop and had what conversation he wanted with the king, and then went homeward. When he had come east to Canterbury he took a meal and his men too, and went on to Dover. When he was a mile or so on this side of Dover he put on his armour and so did all his men, and marched to Dover. When they got there they wanted to take lodgings where they fancied. Then one of his men came and wanted to stop at a man's house against his will, and he wounded the householder, and the householder slew him. Then Eustace mounted his horse and his men theirs and went to that householder and slew him by his own fireside, and then went up to the citadel and slew more than twenty men either inside it or outside. Then the townsmen slew nineteen men on the other side and wounded they didn't know how many. And Eustace broke away with a few men and went to the king and told him a one-sided story of how he had fared. And the king was enraged against the townspeople. And the king sent for Earl Godwine and bade him go to Kent and make war on Dover, for Eustace had told the king that it was more the townspeople's fault than his, but it was not so. And the earl was unwilling to agree to that expedition for he found it hateful to destroy his own people.   PETERBOROUGH CHRONICLE, anno 1048

So the story told by the Canterbury chronicler begins, and one can feel his local patriotism; he emphasises the horror of a man being struck down by a foreigner by his own hearth; he punctures Eustace's false story to the king by his plaintive aside: 'But it was not so.' Yet a northern version of the *Chronicle* gives another side to the story. Earl Godwine's own behaviour was not above reproach, and after all Eustace was a guest in the country. Together they go to show how far the art of prose writing had progressed by the eve of the Norman Conquest. But the earlier parts, too, are not without extended passages of comparable merit. Because the *Chronicle* is called the *Chronicle* throughout its length it is easy to forget that it is a patchwork compilation, even including seven poems, drawing on many sources in the earlier part, and kept up to date over a couple of centuries in the various places to which copies had been sent. At its lowest, the *Chronicle* is a ragbag primarily of interest to the historian; at its highest, as in the Eustace episode or in any of several other episodes, it is a very considerable achievement, approaching that of the prose sagas of Iceland.

ÆLFRIC

The *Chronicle* continued all the while, but it was not until the second half of the century after Alfred that there was another comparable flowering of prose writing. Alfred's work was a response to crisis. The centres of learning in the North had been destroyed during a century of increasing Viking attacks, and, though Western Mercia had escaped the worst ravages, learning was at a very low ebb when Alfred came to the throne. He made his translations so that all freeborn boys should have a chance to learn something in their own language to form a basis from which a smaller number could go on and learn Latin. It took the best part of a century for the revival of learning to bear full fruit and this could not have happened without the revival of English monastic life which began in the middle of the 10th century with St. Dunstan at Glastonbury, and gained impetus and royal approval in the reign of Edgar (959–75). By the end of the century centres of learning were again well established throughout southern England, and from them came a new spate of prose writing, chiefly religious in tone but not exclusively monastic. Byrhtferth produced his manual in 1011 for the guidance of parish clergy. Ælfric wrote his homilies to provide sermons for less educated priests to preach, and other devotional writings at the request of laymen. Wulfstan, whom we come to next, called the whole nation to repentance.

Much of the prose of this new revival, then, has a different purpose. Alfredian prose was meant for instruction; its main aim was to convey information, and our example from the later part of the *Chronicle* shows how this tradition continued. This new prose was meant to persuade, to alter its hearers. It is the prose of a preacher in the pulpit, not of a scholar in a classroom or study.

Its most noted exponent was Ælfric. He was a monk, educated under Bishop Æthelwold, who with Dunstan was one of the leaders of the monastic revival, at the cathedral monastery at Winchester. In about 987 he was sent to a new monastery at Cerne Abbas in Dorset where he took charge of the school and won for himself a wide reputation for learning. From this period in his life comes much of his English writing. Thus unlike Alfred, who was a self-taught layman, Ælfric had had a full clerical education, and had spent years teaching others. He could not but be influenced by medieval rhetorical theory which taught that writing could be used for three purposes: instruction, entertainment and moving the emotions, and that each of these had its own appropriate style, the plain, the middle and the elevated. Now Alfred had developed a good plain style for instructional prose built on the rhythms of everyday speech. This could hardly be bettered. What was needed was an equivalent of the Latin elevated style, since the rhetorical devices based on the Latin periodic sentence were not available for use in English. Classical Latin orators used a system of rhythmical endings (*clausulae*), which followed the patterns of verse. Some medieval writers introduced rhyme into their Latin prose, and Celtic writers in particular had a tendency to highly ornate and intricate Latin. Ælfric's new English high style draws upon native poetic traditions, borrowing chiefly its rhythmical patterns and alliteration, while ignoring the entire poetic vocabulary.

This does not mean that Ælfric did not write plainly and simply when occasion demanded. His instructional works are as direct and straightforward as Alfred's. Alliterative prose would be out of place in such works as his grammar or his *De Temporibus Anni*, just as the prose of an underground newspaper would be in a technical handbook today. With this in mind, we can pass over his educational works and turn to those in which he is trying to persuade as well as teach.

First appearances are not very enticing; his major works consist of three series of 40 sermons each and of translations from the Old Testament. And while the Bible still sells well even today, sermons no longer have the attraction they had in the 19th century. But Ælfric was a born teacher; he had a gift for exposition and there are far worse sermons being preached Sunday by Sunday today. The first two series are called *Catholic Homilies* and the third *Lives of the Saints*, but the distinction is more apparent than real. They are all pieces suitable for delivery to a congregation on the appropriate day in the liturgical year, and all three series have both homilies and saints' lives in them. They are not however original. Ælfric is largely working from other Latin sources, Bede, Jerome, Gregory, Augustine, whom he acknowledges. But in his process of distilling the wisdom of the Fathers for the use of his countrymen he adapts and alters so much as to make almost new pieces out of them.

The first series, dating from 989, largely expounds the scriptures; the second some three years later is beginning to move away from straight teaching towards the story-telling with a moral, that is the feature of the later *Lives of the Saints*. In this series the legendary is so much in evidence as to foreshadow the later medieval tales of wonder. His prose also develops through the three series. In the first it is normally simple and direct, and there is only a little rhythmic or alliterative prose for special effect. In the second and third series the language becomes more ornate as the plain teaching becomes less. It is so marked that some editors have printed some of the lives as verse, but it is not verse; it is a strongly rhythmical prose employing alliteration, more incantation than speech. This auditory quality makes it almost impossible to give extended examples here: too much is lost in translation:

He sent then to Scotland where the faith then was, and asked the elders to grant his request, and send him some teacher to entice his people to God, and this was granted him. They soon then sent to the saintly king a certain worthy bishop, Aidan by name.

THE LIFE OF KING OSWALD

Anyone who compares this with the original will see the strain of finding words to alliterate, but they will also see that we have had to alter the sentence structure and word order comparatively little. Ælfric, though he ended his life as the first abbot of Eynsham near Oxford from 1005 onwards, was at heart a teacher and noted grammarian; he had too much care for language to distort its natural flow too far in a search for special effects. Not for nothing have his homilies been described as 'the classic example of Anglo-Saxon prose'.

WULFSTAN

Unlike Ælfric, Wulfstan, our last subject, has the fire of a Welsh revivalist preacher. Little is known of his origins; when he is heard of first he is already Bishop of London and noted for his preaching. From 1002 to his death in 1023 he was Archbishop of York and until 1016 concurrently Bishop of Worcester. He was heavily involved in secular affairs under the two kings Æthelred and Cnut in whose laws his hand can be seen. But important as his legal work is, his fame rests chiefly on one blistering sermon which he addressed to the whole English people in 1014 (*Sermo Lupi ad Anglos*). Just as a Welsh priest, Gildas, whom he mentions, had excoriated the British five hundred years before, showing that the Saxon invasions were God's punishment for their sinful ways, so too Wulfstan invokes the Danish invaders as evidence for the sinfulness of the English, whose sins he lists at length. He employs an impassioned prose, strongly rhythmical, alliterative and full of parallelisms in a way that goes far beyond Ælfric's own elevated style:

Lo! we know full well that a great sin requires great satisfaction, and a great fire no little water if a man is to quite quench it. And great is the need for every man to eagerly observe God's law henceforward better than he did before, and duly perform his duty to God.   SERMO LUPI AD ANGLOS

Fifty years later the Normans came, and it was almost another two centuries after that before an English king addressed his people in their own language, when in 1258 Henry II issued a proclamation in English, the first official document in English since the Conquest.

4

Poetry

The almost universal use of prose as a literary medium today makes it hard to realise that it has not always been so. 'Writer' now means 'prose writer'; the bulk of imaginative writing is done in prose, while verse, apart from recent manifestations such as the Barrow Poets who have taken poetry to the pub, has become very much a private affair. So much so that attempts by Eliot, Fry and others to bring verse back to the theatre seem to have something of a contradiction in terms about them. The shift from verse to prose has been only gradual; it has been going on for centuries, and the victory of prose is still comparatively modern. It was finally achieved by the development of the prose novel in the 18th century. Thus the restricted range of Old English prose, which we have already noted, means that verse had a far more important role, particularly as the medium for entertainment, but not exclusively so.

Our knowledge of Old English poetry is at best fragmentary, and much of the little that remains has come down to us in an incomplete, corrupt or illegible state. But although the earliest surviving poetry dates only from the 7th century, the piecing together of information from early historians, and from the surviving poetry itself, gives us a clear picture of a long oral tradition stemming from the practices of the German tribes several centuries before they came to these shores. One of the earliest of these hints is in the *Germania* of Tacitus, where he records that the Germans used verse to record their history, to commemorate their heroes and to give courage in battle.

Songs, however, did not merely serve as chronicles for un-lettered men. In the long evenings when people were obliged to create their own entertainment, the singing of songs by professional minstrels or by members of the company was a popular pastime. Kingsley Amis's Lucky Jim was a modern fictional sufferer in somewhat bizarre circumstances; Cædmon an actual one in the 7th century. He was a lay brother at Whitby under Abbess Hilda (657–680) when the incident related by Bede occurred, and he received the gift of improvising poetry. (Bede's Latin merely has *cantare*, to sing, but improvisation is demanded by the context.)

Having followed the secular life until he was well on in years Cædmon had never learned any songs. And so often at a feast when it had been decided that everyone should sing in turn to provide entertainment he used to get up in the middle of the proceedings when he saw the harp getting near him, and go out back to his house.

On one occasion when he had done this and had left the place where the feast was he went to the stables because he was on duty that night in charge of the beasts. When the time came he lay down to sleep, and in a dream saw someone standing at his side who greeted him and called him by name: 'Cædmon, sing me something.' Cædmon replied: 'I don't know how to sing. I left the feast and came out here because I could not sing.' Again the speaker addressed him: 'But you must sing to me.' 'What must I sing?' 'Sing about the Creation of all things.' As soon as he had heard this Cædmon began to sing verses which he had never heard before in honour of God the Creator. . . . When he woke up he remembered all that he had sung while he was asleep, and soon added more verses in the same style in praise of God.

Bede HIST. ECCL. IV. xxiv

Cædmon's poems were all on religious themes, though only the tiny fragment of his first poem which is found in some manuscripts of Bede can confidently be ascribed to him. He felt, Bede says, that his was a gift from God that should not be wasted on secular, let alone profane subjects. Other clergy were less scrupulous; like the Salvation Army they did not see why the Devil should have all the best tunes. In the 7th century Aldhelm, according to William of Malmesbury, the post-Conquest historian, attracted a congregation for his sermons by first singing popular songs by the roadside. These have not survived, so that the orthodox have had the last laugh. But Alcuin's rebuke, which we have already met in the first chapter, to the monks of Lindisfarne for listening to heroic lays in the refectory instead of stories from scripture, should serve to remind us of how ingrained the use of song for entertainment was, and that the mere fact of entering a cloister does not automatically kill worldly tastes. Throughout *Beowulf* the recital of poetry is associated with leisure and revelry. On many occasions when the warriors are feasting and the ale-cup is passed round, the minstrel is there to entertain the assembly. Even as the Geats ride away from the mere after Beowulf has overcome Grendel's mother, songs of rejoicing are sung—Tacitus's verse chronicles in the making.

Another indication of how common story-telling in verse was before the days of literacy is the frequency of allusions to other stories in the poetry that has survived. Most of these historical and legendary names now mean very little to us, which makes a poem like *Widsith* difficult to appreciate. We have been brought up on Classical mythology; Zeus or Jupiter evoke a bigger response than Odin or Wotan, Hercules and Oedipus than Beowulf and Sigurd. The audience of these poems, on the other hand, must have been familiar with all the tales and exploits attached to these names, and have learnt about them by listening to lays sung by minstrels in the mead-hall or the market-place. The lists of names in *Widsith*, like the headwords to a *Who's Who* of Germanic legend, give us some idea of the repertoire of stories that were at the command of the Anglo-Saxon minstrel or *scop* (*scop* = 'shaper', compare Greek *poetes* = 'maker' or Scots *makar*). The number of names that mean little or nothing to us now is a measure of how much has been lost, for the poet refers not only to Germanic legend but to Greeks, Burgundians and Israelites as well. The poem, then, is valuable to a search for information about the earliest poetry by suggesting the sort of subject that was in demand—tales of past battles and of mighty heroes—but also by throwing some light on the position of wandering minstrels and the rewards they earned by their song:

The lord of the Myrgings gave me land, my father's home, and then Ealhild, a noble and worthy queen, the daughter of Eadwin, gave me another. Her praise has spread throughout many countries, whenever I had opportunity to tell in my song where I best knew under the heavens a richly adorned queen bestowing gifts. When Schilling and I with a clear voice raised up a song before our victorious lord, loudly to the accompaniment of the harp played in harmony, then many proud-spirited men said that they well knew that they had never heard anything better.   WIDSITH 95–108

Deor is another poem about a minstrel. But whereas Widsith, as his name, Far-traveller, implies, wanders from court to court, Deor remains in the service of one master. The poem is a lament about the loss of his estate because another has taken his position as court *scop*. In a series of stanzas linked by the haunting refrain: 'That has passed away; this may too' (Þæs oferode, þisses swa mæg), he relates five traditional stories of misfortunes that did not last for ever, ending:

Once I was the minstrel of the Heodenings and well loved by my lord. My name was Deor. For many years my master was well disposed to me and I prospered, until now Heorrenda, a man skilled in song, has received the privileges of land which the protector of nobles formerly granted to me.

That has passed away; this may too.   DEOR 36–42

The subject-matter of the surviving poetry reinforces the picture of the position of the minstrel and the function of poetry which we have already gathered from glimpses of *scops* in action in the poems: that it was composed for recitation at court for an audience such as that depicted in *Beowulf*, the king and queen, their thanes and counsellors. The world of these poems is that of the more affluent and sophisticated members of Anglo-Saxon Society.

Beowulf, as befits a heroic poem, is filled with descriptions of courtly customs, ornate armour, banquets, and speeches expressing high regard for duty and honour. The 'lower classes' are conspicuous by their absence. Their only representative, the runaway serf who discovers the hidden treasure, points up by his uniqueness how aristocratic the world of the poem is. And it is true even of other *genres*; elegies like *The Wanderer* and *The Seafarer* tell of men who have fallen out of favour with their lords and lost all their possessions. To have had so much to lose and to have been formerly so close to their lord implies that they were not herdsmen or labourers but rather thanes or counsellors. The same atmosphere is found even in paraphrases from the Bible. The Israelites encamped in *Exodus* are not far removed from the English army at Maldon; the Hebrews in *Daniel* 'distributed treasure' like any Germanic leader. Even the style and tone of the poetry point to an aristocratic audience, and although it would not be wise to lay too much stress on the argument it could be said that the formal conventions and abundance of repetitions give the poetry a stately and dignified pace suitable for a stately and dignified audience.

This stress on the aristocratic nature of the surviving poetry does not mean that there was no popular verse. On the contrary, we know that it existed; the stories of Cædmon and Aldhelm prove as much. But none has survived. If it had we would have been in a better position to judge just how 'upper class' is the poetry we have. Thus the loss of the popular songs of an Aldhelm is greater than their intrinsic value alone. As it is, whether the common people also sang and enjoyed the aristocratic verse, or whether it is because the clergy thought parchment too precious to be wasted on recording such matter that all record of their poetry has been lost over the centuries must remain a mystery.

It is certainly not difficult to explain the popularity of the minstrels and their songs. England at that time was heavily forested, with wolf-infested woodlands and swampy marshes. Communications were not of the easiest, certainly worse than under the Romans because of the disrepair of the Roman road system, and many men would have little chance to travel and experience the world for themselves. The simile of the sparrow in Bede shows that the hall was an oasis of life, warmth and colour in a hostile world:

> If we compare the present earthly life of man with that time of which we have no knowledge, it seems to me like when you are sitting at the feast in winter with your elders and thanes with a fire

> burning in the centre to warm the hall while outside rage wintry
> storms of snow and rain, and a lone sparrow flies swiftly through the
> hall. It comes in at one door and quickly flies out through another.
> While it is inside, the wintry tempest cannot touch it, but after the
> briefest moment of calm it goes back into the storm from which it
> came and is lost to sight. Bede HIST. ECCL. II. xiii

Thus one of the counsellors of King Edwin of Northumbria in 627, presumably at Yeavering on the northern foothills of the Cheviot, not the most hospitable site for a palace. It is a setting like this that we must imagine for poems like *Beowulf*, with the minstrel an honoured figure in that oasis of comfort, an honoured figure who could with his tales of heroes and far-off days make these now settled people feel part of the glorious tradition of their Germanic ancestry and nomadic past.

It is clear that the earliest poetry was conveyed orally. What has survived to this day could be likened to the tip of the iceberg which shows a mass of ice above water but hides beneath the surface quantities that can scarcely be guessed at. To complicate matters further it is more than probable that what remains gives only a distorted picture of Old English poetry as a whole. Literacy was confined to the clergy; they were the scribes who wrote the manuscripts in which the poetry is preserved. It is natural, as Cædmon's scruples suggest, that they would have been more inclined to pass over flippant or pagan material for poetry with a Christian or moral content, particularly adaptations of Bible stories or lives of saints. Therefore it is the *preservation* of heroic poems like *Beowulf*, not their loss, which needs an explanation. The most convincing explanation is a monkish weakness for the traditional heroic lay as entertainment, as may be shown by Alcuin's needing to send a rebuke to Lindisfarne. But however many manuscripts came to be written, we can be sure that large numbers perished in the storming and sacking of the monasteries that began with the Viking raids and the loss of the library at Jarrow, one of the finest in Western Europe, and which were only ended by the final dissolution of the monasteries in the 16th century under Henry VIII. Even so the tale of destruction is not over. When we think how narrowly two of the best surviving Old English poems, *Beowulf* and *The Battle of Maldon*, reached the 20th century—the former had its edges singed in 1731 in a fire that could easily have destroyed it completely, and the latter was probably only written down in the first place because Byrhtnoth, its hero, was a man of importance and a generous and staunch protector of monasteries—we are left to wonder how many more poems were never committed to writing, or were used over the years to kindle fires, line cupboards, bind more 'valuable' volumes, wrap up meat, or stop draughts. It would have taken the loss of only another four manuscripts to have deprived us of virtually all Old English poetry; and we must remember that the cult of the manuscript is a modern phenomenon. Only recently have poets been able to sell to American universities the contents of their wastepaper baskets for more than the publication of the finished poems could possibly bring them.

VERSIFICATION

Before discussing the style and techniques of Old English poetry it is essential to have some grasp of the Old English metric conventions, and to see where they differ from other more familiar conventions. After all, as far as the outward form goes, verse is very much a matter of convention. What distinguishes it from prose is the superimposition of a recognised pattern, the convention, upon the natural flow of the words. In Hebrew verse it takes the form of parallelism of expression, which is familiar enough from the Psalms, though not perhaps always recognised as a form of verse, particularly by those whose Bibles do not set it out in lines as verse. Another pattern, more rigid, is the Japanese *haiku* with its seventeen syllables arranged in three lines of five, seven and five each.

In Europe there have been three main traditions of versification. The one with the oldest surviving verse is that of Classical Greek and Latin. This is quantitative verse; the length of syllables is counted, and they are arranged in patterns of long (–) and short (⌣), almost like Morse code, with the long in theory taking twice as long to pronounce as the short. One could in fact transmit the metre of any Classical poem without the words as Morse code. However, it cannot be reproduced exactly in English because we do not have the same sense of length of syllable. One attempt is Tennyson's 'Oh you chorus of indolent reviewers', a pastiche of hendecasyllabics, a lyric metre ($- - - \cup\cup - \cup - \cup - \cup$). The arrangement of syllables into patterns of long and short produces a basic rhythm, which in narrative metres escapes monotony by the use of permitted variations, and the counterpoint of this rhythm against the basic speech rhythms brings the verse to life.

In the languages which grew out of Latin, this scansion of long and short syllables developed into counting the number not the weight of syllables in a line whose end was marked by rhyme. Here tension comes from the sense of the verse flowing on over the end of the line. The French influence at court after the Conquest, followed by the Classical renaissance, made this the commonest verse form in English. The Alexandrine 'That like a wounded snake drags its slow length along' (Pope) may be rare in English, but most of our poetry from the ballads onwards is based on scansion of this type. It is too common to need further description.

The third form of versification depends not on quantity as the Classical does, nor on syllable counting, but on accent; that is on the relative stress placed on syllables, not on the time taken to utter them. The number of syllables is not fixed, but is held in bounds by the natural proportion of stressed to unstressed syllables. There is no place for that young man from Japan 'whose limericks never would scan'. Strange as it may seem, the earliest Latin verse was of this type, but by the Classical period it had almost completely been supplanted by Greek models, just as French models won the day in this country: both languages were felt to have cultural superiority.

This third pattern is common to the early Germanic languages, but we shall here discuss only the English form. The Old English verse line was divided into two half-lines. (In early editions they were often printed as separate lines, thus giving the verse an entirely different look on the page.) Each half-line had two stressed syllables, and a variable number of unstressed syllables, with a third lighter stress as well in some cases. Rhyme is found very rarely; the necessary discipline being provided by alliteration which is used to link the stressed syllables of two half-lines together. The rules of alliteration are strictly observed. While any vowel may alliterate with any other vowel (for example, *ancient*, *old* and *elder* alliterate by the rules of Old English versification), consonants must alliterate exactly; *t* can alliterate only with *t*, and not with *d* or *th* which are formed in a similar way in the mouth; *sc* (pronounced *sh*) can alliterate only with *sc* and not with *sp* or *st*. However, some letters are pronounced in several ways according to the phonetic context, and this does not prevent them alliterating with each other.

Stress falls chiefly on nouns, adjectives, infinitives, numerals, and participles. If there are not enough of these in the line to make up the proper stress pattern, then verbs and adverbs may take a stress. Pronouns, prepositions, conjunctions and interjections are hardly ever stressed. One of the stresses of the first half-line must alliterate with the first stress of the second half-line. Both stresses of the first half-line may alliterate; the final stress of the second half rarely does. As an illustration, here is a short riddle, first in the original and then in a translation by Michael Alexander which attempts to reproduce the form as well as the content of the verse:

Moþþe word fræt;   me þæt þuhte
wrætlicu wyrd,   þa ic þæt wundor gefrægn,
þæt se wyrm forswealg   wera gied sumes,
þeof in þystro   brymfæstne cwide
and þæs strangan staþol: stælgiest ne wæs
wihte þy gleawra   þe he þam wordum swealg.

EXETER BOOK: RIDDLE 47

I heard a wonder, of words moth-eaten;
that is a strange thing, I thought, weird
that a man's song be swallowed by a worm,

> his binded sentences, his bedside stand-by
> rustled in the night—and the robber-guest
> not one whit the wiser for the words he had mumbled.

[The answer incidentally is a 'bookworm'.]

We are unable to reconstruct satisfactorily the way in which these poems were recited. There is no doubt the harp played a part in the rendering of the poem, but we still know little about the Anglo-Saxon harp and the extent to which it was used in recitation. Nor are we certain just what instrument we mean by 'harp', and the help offered by archaeology is not entirely straightforward. Fragments of instruments have been found, at Sutton Hoo just before the war and at Taplow. But instead of these discoveries confirming the impression that harps were common instruments, they have had a rather unsettling effect. Why have only two been found? The wood of course is liable to decay, but metal facings and other parts could be expected to have survived. Yet no trace has been found in the big cemeteries in Kent and in the Thames valley where one might have expected fairly numerous finds. Perhaps they were not as common as was thought. Nor is this the only uncertainty. Work could not start in earnest on the finds from Sutton Hoo until after the war, but already the fragments have been reconstructed twice as two different stringed instruments of the harp or lyre type.

The evidence of the literature itself, on the other hand, seems quite clear. Harps were used as a part of the recitation of verse. We have already quoted the story of Cædmon; he went off before the harp reached him as it was passed round the company as each man took his turn at singing. Widsith sings 'loudly to the accompaniment of the harp played in harmony'. In *Beowulf* Grendel's rest was disturbed by the revelry in hall where 'there was the sound of the harp, the clear song of the minstrel'. In *The Fates of Men* the *scop* sits and sings at court: 'One shall sit at his lord's feet with his harp, receive treasure and ever swiftly sweep the strings, let the leaping plectrum sound aloud, the finger nail with its melody.' Other examples would be superfluous but not hard to find. But how the harp was used remains a mystery. We do not know if it was played all the time, with the words fitting into the rhythm that it set, if it was strummed in the pauses, or if it was used to highlight important or emotional passages such as the elegy of the sole survivor or the father's lament in *Beowulf*.

We gain no help from later poetry either. Old English versification survived until the 14th century in a degenerate form, but both the language itself and social conditions had changed, and the old alliterative stressed style became submerged in the gradual process of cultural change brought about by closer and closer contact with the continent. Its last flowering is perhaps Langland's *Piers Plowman*:

> A faire felde ful of folke · fonde I there bytwene,
> Of alle maner of men · þe mene and þe riche,
> Worchyng and wandryng · as þe worlde asketh. . . .
> And somme murthes to make · as mynstralles conneth,
> And geten gold with here glee · synneles, I leue.

17ff.

Minstrels, of course, are always with us even if they change their title; styles change too, and even the 14th century is too late to help us with the problem of the Anglo-Saxon harp. After *Piers Plowman* the change from alliterative verse is virtually complete. English metre was no longer measured in half-lines; English poets imitated the continental, originally Classical, practice of counting syllables. The Classical long syllable was represented by a stressed syllable, and the short by an unstressed, and the accented form of the iambic pentameter held the field for centuries. In Chaucer we can see the beginnings of this type of verse. The iambic foot x / is the most common pattern in his verse, but it can also be read as stressed verse, depending upon your theories of Chaucerian versification. After Chaucer there is no doubt that the iambic line is the standard, and this 'Common English Metre' so dominates the verse we learn from nursery rhymes in the cradle onwards, that any other system seems strange. However, the importance of Old English versification is what it does to the poetry, and this we turn to next. The details of the technique itself can better be derived from other sources, perhaps most succinctly from J. R. R. Tolkien's introduction to the Clark Hall translation of *Beowulf*.

For the modern reader with generations of literacy behind him, it is very difficult to get on satisfactory terms with the work of the Anglo-Saxon minstrel, who was unable to read, and sang his songs to a live audience. Such composition needs techniques quite different from that of the poetry which is first written down and intended to be read, whether to an audience or silently by the reader to himself. Obviously the minstrel must aim at holding his listeners' attention all the time; if it lapses they may never regain the thread of the story. He must aim at a flowing, lucid delivery, and at smoothly connected sequences of thought; he cannot permit himself that sort of obscurity which T. S. Eliot calls 'the suppression of links in the chain', and of which his *Waste Land* is a supreme example. Since our evidence suggests that many of these songs were extempore, with the minstrel composing as he went along—immediately after Beowulf has disposed of Grendel the minstrel celebrates his feat—we may be tempted to look on the early poets as some sort of miracle men. But in this case faith is not required; partly, it seems, a memory that has not atrophied through its owner's reliance on books can cope with poems of this length; partly the special tricks of oral poetry make feats of memory possible. One well-documented example (the poem was recorded) came from a sixty-year-old bard in Jugoslavia in 1934. This man, who could neither read nor write, recited to Professor Milman Parry a poem of some 12,000 lines, or the length of the *Odyssey*. He made it up as he went along, all the time retaining metre and form without losing track of a complicated narrative. The whole performance lasted for two weeks of two two-hour sessions daily with a break of a week in the middle. Similar feats have been attested in other parts of the world, including the British Isles.

But even given the advantage of a memory unspoilt by literacy, it would be impossible for anyone to compose so spontaneously without aids to help him out when his imagination flagged, or when it was hard to fit what he wanted to say into the appropriate metre. To help the poet in circumstances like this a mass of formulaic expressions was built up over the centuries, to provide precedents or a spur to the memory. The formulae comprise a variety of phrases and epithets in regular rhythmical patterns, which were at hand whenever the situation required. This is true of any oral poetry; formulae are as characteristic of Homer as they are of *Beowulf*. Often when a warrior is in warlike mood he brandishes his spear or shield before speaking. So Hrothgar's watchman sees Beowulf and his men approaching and shakes his mighty spear-shaft as he asks them their business. So too Byrhtnoth in *The Battle of Maldon* often brandishes his shield as he urges his men into battle. This is but one example from heroic poetry; another set of formulae is found in the elegies, signifying deprivation, telling how the speaker has lost all that was dear to him. The Wanderer is *eðle bidæled* (deprived of his native land) and *dreame bidorene* (deprived of joy); in *Genesis* Adam is *duguðum bedæled* (deprived of retainers), and in the elegiac passage in *Beowulf* containing the lament of the sole survivor of the treasure we can see it again in the sentence: 'Now will the hard helmet adorned with gold be deprived of ornament.' The special demands of alliteration have added many phrases to this store. *Heard under helme* (brave in his armour) is common in *Beowulf*, and throughout the surviving heroic poems are tags such as *yrre ond anræd* (angry and resolute), *ord ond ecg* (spear point and blade) or *habban ond healdan* (have and hold), stock alliterating phrases ready to help fill out a line.

Whilst encouraging the development of numerous stereotyped words and phrases, Old English poetry is also prone to variation and the wide use of synonyms. This may seem paradoxical. Why, one may ask, should a style which demands the frequent occurrence of similar phrases—three-quarters of the first fifty half-lines in *Beowulf* have parallels elsewhere—also demand the contrary practice of conveying the same idea in different ways? One reason is that by repeating what he has just said the minstrel allows himself time to think how to phrase the next part of his song. Alliteration provides another, and caused an accumulation of synonyms as well as of formulae to make it easier to find a word to fit into a given pattern of alliteration. For example, *þengel, fengel, þeoden, aldor, brego, eodor, þeod cyning, landfruma, ordfruma, ræswa* are all used in the poetry for 'prince' or 'leader'. But it would be wise all the same to keep some reservations about the synonymity of all these. The linguistic and social gaps between modern and pre-Conquest English mean that we may not now be able to discern the shades of meaning that could have given each of these a slightly different significance of its own. Yet the same process can be seen at work with proper names. In *Beowulf* the Danes are called variously *Beorht-Dene, Gar-Dene, Hring-Dene, Norð-Dene* and *East-Dene*, and although none of the first elements of the compounds are synonymous (far from it in the case of *East* and *North*), yet the compounds as a whole are used as names of the same people, presumably to accommodate the demands of metre or alliteration.

There is a valuable passage in *Beowulf* where we can see how some of the techniques of oral poetry were put to work. Beowulf has just killed the monster, Grendel; without being forewarned, and with no opportunity for preparation, the minstrel composes a lay to commemorate the deed:

> At times [as they rode back from the mere to which the monster's tracks had led them] one of the king's thanes, a warrior who could sing well, who remembered heroic tales and could call to mind a great many traditions, formed a new story with words correctly linked; the man began to recite with skill the adventure of Beowulf, to tell successfully an appropriate tale, and to vary his words.
>
> 867–874

Notice that last phrase 'to vary his words'. It can only refer to the use of formulae and synonyms. Let *Beowulf* itself provide an example:

> Men carried *bright decorated weapons, splendid armour* into the hollow of the ship. The *warriors*, the *men* on their eager journey pushed off the well-timbered ship. Then the foamy prowed boat driven by the wind went over the billowy sea just like a bird, until in due time on

the next day the ship with the curved prow had come so far that the sailors could see the *land*, the *sea-cliffs* glistening, the *steep hills*, the *broad promontories*.   213–223

In the best Old English poetry this parallelism is not merely the plain restatement of an idea. The poet uses it to emphasise, specialise or generalise, or to enrich his audience's understanding of what he is trying to convey. In the last passage the plain term 'land' is amplified and different aspects of the land as seen from a ship brought to our attention. The whole is a decided enrichment of our perception of the land. But the use of variation does hold back the pace of the poetry, though even this can be turned to advantage. One example might be Grendel's approach to Heorot, the hall where Beowulf and his men are sleeping. Tension is sustained, as in a long shot of the hero slowly striding down the deserted main street in a Western. Another is Beowulf's own approach to the mere where the fatally wounded Grendel has taken refuge:

Then the sons of nobles traversed the steep and rocky slopes, the narrow paths, the thin lonely tracks—an unknown way—precipitous cliffs, many dwellings of water monsters. With a few skilled men he went on ahead to view the region, until suddenly he discovered mountain trees overhanging a grey rock, a joyless forest. The water was beneath, blood-stained and turbulent.   1408–1417

The progress of the warriors is shown to be slow and difficult, and their gloom and fear to be mounting, by the listing of obstacle after obstacle, each half-line conveying a further significant detail in the description of the narrow rocky path. But the device could be hard to handle, and sometimes has the effect merely of clogging up the train of the narrative. It seems a pity to have to criticise a piece like Cædmon's *Hymn*, early as it is, and with a splendid circumstantial story attached to it, but it can be said to contain nothing but a string of words and phrases standing for God, which contribute little but bulk to the poem. As Milman Parry once remarked, one poet is better than another not because he has by himself found a more striking way of expressing his own thought, but because he has been able to make better use of a tradition.

The passage used to illustrate variation also contains several circumlocutions for 'ship'. These are examples of another feature of Old English poetic style, the descriptive compound, or 'kenning'. A ship may be called *wægflota* (floater on the waves), *hringed-stefna* (ring-prowed), *sægenga* (sea goer), or *brimwudu* (seawood); a lord *beaga brytta* (dispenser of rings), *sinces-gifa* (treasure-giver), *goldwine gumena* (generous lord of men), *folces hyrde* (his people's shepherd), *wigendra hleo* (protector of warriors). Compounds are found in all the extant poetry, but the use of the kenning is confined to our earliest verse. 'Kenning' is an Icelandic term, and it was there that it was most highly developed. It may be defined as a metaphoric phrase designed to vary in an interesting way the concept for which it stands. Thus the sea is called *swanrad* (swan's road), *hronrad* (whale's road), *ganotes bæþ* (gannet's bath), *yþa ful* (cup of waves); the sun is called *woruldcandel* (candle of the world), and a ship *mere-hengest* (horse of the sea). Whereas the parallels give the verse a restrained and leisurely pace, the compounds and compressed metaphors of the kennings work the other way and give a great compression of thought, though nothing like the compression, rivalling that of the *haiku*, that the Icelandic poets achieved. Old English poetry used very few similes, but by means of these compounds the poet is able to give the same effect of a multiplicity of associations but with far greater economy of words.

It would be foolish to pretend that Old English poetry is not without its limitations. The highly formal structure, fraught with conventions, and the convenience of ready-made phrases, can easily fall into unthinking monotony, a routine listing of subjects and themes. Still we should not write off the early poetry because some may be open to this criticism. Instead we must meet it on its own ground, understand the thought behind the subjects treated. Because the poetry was originally oral, and because all the conventions were traditional, the poet was obliged to reflect a simplified image of life, depicting for example the conflict of good and evil, a conflict which is structurally reenacted by the balanced half-lines of the verse and by its alliteration. With the exception of some riddles and gnomic verse, the Old English poetry that has survived is either heroic, religious or elegiac; in the following chapters we shall examine how successfully the early poets put the various conventions to work.

5

Beowulf and Heroic Poetry

In *Beowulf* Old English has a story which has been judged worthy of retelling for children. This great epic therefore finds itself classed with other stories like Homer's *Iliad* and *Odyssey* or the legends of Greece, Rome and Scandinavia. And it is a stirring tale of adventure, of good subduing evil, of monsters and dragons and treasure. But as with many childhood favourites there is more to it than just a good story. Consider how the great classics of children's literature have new depths for the adult reader; or better still, re-read one, *Alice in Wonderland* or *The Wind in the Willows* for instance, if you have not done so lately, and then remember that *Beowulf* was not composed as a children's tale, but only later has been found to contain the makings of one. If we keep this in mind we should find it easier not to lose sight of what sometimes may seem to be all too easily forgotten, and that is that *Beowulf*, whatever else the poet may have had in mind, is a poem for entertainment.

But *Beowulf* is only one, although the longest and best known, of a number of poems which can conveniently be grouped together. These are:

1. *Beowulf*, the only surviving epic, generally regarded as the best Old English poem.
2. *Waldere*, a fragment which is all that remains of an epic which some think might have rivalled *Beowulf* in length and artistry.
3. *Widsith*, an early poem; not so much a heroic poem in itself, as one that shows something of the world of heroic poetry and its makers.

4. *The Fight at Finnesburg*, another incomplete poem, notable for its truly heroic spirit.
5. Two later poems about actual events in the 10th-century wars against the Danes: *The Battle of Maldon* and *The Battle of Brunanburh*.

The subject of *Beowulf* is the hero's three encounters with monsters; it falls into two parts. In the first, Beowulf, a Geat from what is now southern Sweden, hears that Hrothgar, the Danish king, is being troubled by a monster named Grendel, who, annoyed by the sounds of revelry, attacks the royal hall by night and slaughters many of the warriors. Beowulf, strong and fearless, goes to Denmark to help the king; he kills Grendel with little difficulty. Thereupon there is jubilation amongst the Danes, and great festivities are held. But that night a second monster comes. It is Grendel's mother who avenges her son by carrying off Æschere, the king's most favoured thane. In the morning Beowulf follows the tracks to her lair at the bottom of a mere where they fight for hours amidst mounds of jewels and other treasure, but in the end Beowulf is victorious. After more celebrations and the presentation of rich rewards, Beowulf returns home.

In the second part of the poem, Beowulf is an old man who has been an ideal king of the Geats for fifty years. News comes that a dragon, who was guarding a hoard of buried treasure, has been roused to fury by a runaway serf who had stumbled across it and taken a goblet. In an attempt to recover his lost treasure, the dragon is storming through the kingdom spreading fire and destruction. Beowulf immediately sets out with a band of followers to slay the monster. In a fierce and fiery encounter, in which all his companions but the faithful Wiglaf desert him, Beowulf, grievously wounded, kills the dragon and dies himself.

Beowulf is over 3000 lines long; the two fragments of *Waldere*, which survived by chance when the vellum on which they were written was used to bind another manuscript, are only a fiftieth of this. Their interest lies more in speculation about what might have been, than in merit of their own. Had more survived, it would probably have been another matter entirely. *Widsith*, which we have already mentioned in the last chapter, is another tantalising piece, in which the poet recounts his travels and his repertoire. If nothing else, it is some indication of how much poetry must have been lost.

The fragment of *The Fight at Finnesburg*, which survives only in an 18th-century transcript of a single leaf from the Lambeth Palace Library, now vanished, tells part of the story of the visit of the Danish king, Hnæf, to Frisia. After a quarrel the Danes defend themselves for five days until the Frisians withdraw. A stalemate follows an unsuccessful sortie, until one of the Danes called Hengest—probably the invader of Kent—agrees that the Danish remnant will serve King Finn, Hnæf being dead by now. In the spring the Danes return home, but come back to avenge Hnæf despite the oaths they had taken when they entered Finn's service. The fragment itself tells only of the five days' defence of a hall; in this the heroic virtues are praised, but much of the rest of the story is told incidentally in *Beowulf*.

With *The Battle of Maldon* and *The Battle of Brunanburh*, we turn from legend to history. These poems, one from *The Anglo-Saxon Chronicle*, commemorate actual battles. The site of Brunanburh where in 937 Athelstan met an invading force of Scots and Vikings is not known, though presumably it is somewhere in the Solway region; but the site of the Battle of Maldon can be localised with a high degree of certainty to the island of Northey in the estuary of the Essex Blackwater near the town of Maldon. Here in 991 Byrhtnoth, the leader of the local militia, faced a force of Vikings encamped on the island. At first he had the upper hand, but then the invaders appealed to his martial spirit and sense of fair play, and he allowed them to cross the causeway which joined the island to the mainland where there was more room for fighting. From this overconfident move stems his death and the defeat of the English. The actual engagement can have had but little effect on the course of the Viking wars, but yet this little band of men have been given the immortality of the great Germanic heroes by this one short poem.

Their brave deeds have truly won them the sort of fame accorded to Leonidas and his Spartans after Thermopylae.

The connection between these poems is the Germanic ethos which we have already described with the help of Tacitus in the second chapter. In all of them the representation of events is dominated by the bond between the lord and his companions. In the opening lines of *Beowulf* this relationship is set before us:

> In this way ought a young man to bring it about by his virtue, by his liberal gifts while he is still under his father's protection, that when he is old dear companions may continue to support him, protect their prince when war comes. 20–24

And at the end, when Beowulf's companions desert him in his extremity for fear of the dragon, his one faithful retainer, Wiglaf, reminds the others of their duty:

> He who wishes to speak the truth may say that the lord who gave you the treasures, the armour which you stand there in—when often at the ale-bench the chieftain distributed to his thanes in hall the trustiest armour he could find anywhere—he completely threw away that war equipment when war befell him. The lord of the people has little need to boast of his comrades in the field. 2864–74

Here we see confirmation of Tacitus's account of the large part played by material benefits in the agreement between the lord and his companions. In return for his service the companion is given horses, armour, a place to live and his lord's protection. He receives his pay for completely loyal service. He must be prepared to fight beside his lord to the death if necessary, and is not expected to leave the field of battle alive if his lord has fallen. (The story of Finn is one of a conflict of obligations arising when this rule is broken.) Any renown which he acquires on his own account must be regarded as bringing glory to his lord; when Beowulf returns home laden with rewards which, however splendid, are small enough in comparison with what he has done, he immediately gives them up willingly to his lord, Hygelac, who had all the time been sitting quietly at home in Geatland. Similarly, elsewhere in the poem, Hygelac is called the slayer of

Ongentheow when it was actually two of his thanes who were responsible for the deed.

But it would be a mistake to consider this bond between lord and companion as callous a one as that which existed amongst Chicago gangsters of the 1920s, with the boss paying high prices to keep his hands clean while his hatchet men do the dirty work. In the Old English relationship there is a high regard for duty and honour which raise it above any such arrangement. The heroic spirit is seen most clearly in the desire for fame and glory both in the warrior's lifetime and after his death. Beowulf voices this sentiment when he consoles the Danish king after Æschere's death:

> Each of us will come to the end of life; he who is able should endeavour to gain glory before his death, for in the end this is best for the departed warrior. 1386-9

And this is what Byrhtnoth and his men won for themselves at Maldon. Here too in a poem commemorating a historical battle loyalty to one's lord is the dominating force:

> Offa was swiftly cut down in the fight; yet he had accomplished what he had promised his lord when he vowed to his benefactor that they should both ride home safely into the stronghold, or both fall in the fight, die from wounds on the battle-field. He lay, as befits a thane, close to his lord.

THE BATTLE OF MALDON 288-94

Nor is this the expected exaggeration of epic poetry; there are comparable passages even in the stark prose of the *Chronicle*. In the year 755, after King Cynewulf had been killed in a night attack, his thanes though greatly outnumbered would not desert his dead body and fought on until only one remained alive. The opposing side were equally courageous; when Cynewulf's main force heard of the attack they surrounded the fort which held the murderers, and offered them safety if they would surrender. They replied that no kinsman was as dear to them as their lord, and they would never follow his slayer; they too died carrying out their duty.

Another aspect of this duty, and one which can likewise be documented from the *Chronicle*, even from the same year, is the taking of lawful revenge on the murderer of a slain companion or kinsman. This was the way in which Anglo-Saxon law dealt with homicide until after the Conquest. When a murder was committed it was the duty of the companions or kin of the victim either to kill his murderer or to obtain from him a material compensation, known as the *wergild*, which varied with the rank of the dead man. The Church did not suppress this practice, but rather encouraged the payment of *wergild*, and preached against the prolonging of a blood-feud yet without whole-hearted disapproval of the taking of vengeance; in 801 Alcuin praised the Northumbrian nobleman, Torhtmund, in a letter to Charlemagne, for having 'boldly avenged the blood of his lord'.

Thus Beowulf's 'Better it is for a man to avenge his friend than mourn much' expresses the honourable attitude to such a situation, a situation which often has the makings of a dramatic conflict. It may be minor; later in the poem Herebald dies from a stray arrow shot from his brother's bow, and his father, Hrethel, finds his son's death especially hard to bear because it must go unavenged; his position is like that of a father who sees his son hanging from the gallows and cannot legally take vengeance on the judge or hangman. A much grittier moral conflict is at the centre of the story of Finn and Hengest which has to be pieced together from *The Fight at Finnesburg* and from the bits which appear in *Beowulf*. The thread is a little difficult to follow because the poet of *Beowulf* assumes that his audience already knows the story well, but the gist seems to be this: Hnæf, accompanied by a band of Danish warriors, is staying with his sister, Hildeburgh, and her husband, Finn, in Frisia. For some reason that is unclear to us a quarrel breaks out, and the Danes take refuge in a hall which they defend successfully for five days. But eventually Hnæf is killed and with him his nephew, Hildeburgh's son. Winter is coming on, and the stormy seas prevent the remainder of Hnæf's men, led now by Hengest, from returning home. And so, forgetting their duty, Hengest and his men compromise in a treaty with Finn by which they become his men. Finn for his part agrees to treat them as equals with his own men provided that they cause no trouble. Hengest's compromise has put him in a spot. Expediency, no doubt, made him swear allegiance to Finn when his troops were well out-numbered and immobilised in a foreign country by the weather. Yet it remains his duty to avenge Hnæf's death, and he is torn between breaking his oath to Finn and his oath to his dead lord. The winter passes quietly, but:

> Then the winter passed by; the bosom of the earth was beautiful. The exiled guest was anxious to be away from the dwellings. Yet he thought more of revenging his injury than of the sea journey.
> BEOWULF 1136-9

In the end Hengest's duty to Hnæf weighs heavier, and in a later raid Finn and many of his warriors with him are killed in revenge.

Another story in *Beowulf* arises from an attempt to end a bloodfeud, which had for years embroiled the Heathobards and the Danes. Hrothgar tried to end it by giving his daughter's hand in marriage to Ingeld the son of Frodo, the Heathobard king. But:

> As a rule seldom at all does the deadly spear lie idle after the downfall of a prince, however good the bride may be.   2029-31

Sure enough, an old warrior who regards the attempt at reconciliation a complete indignity reminds the young warrior of his duty, and hostilities begin again.

So far in discussing the appearance and influence of the Germanic heroic code in English poetry, we have assumed too great a unity of treatment. These poems were composed over a span of four centuries, and it is only reasonable to expect a certain degree of change. The most important agent of change, as we said earlier, was the coming of Christianity. Everything we have has come to us only because a cleric wrote it down, and so everything that has survived has been touched by Christianity to some degree. There is plenty of evidence that purely pagan poetry existed, but what it was like is a harder question. *Waldere* and *The Fight at Finnesburg* are probably nearest to the original Germanic spirit with its proud warlike boasting and real joy in fighting. It is little wonder that they have only come down to us in fragments, the one in the binding of a book, the other on a single leaf, now lost. There is certainly little to warrant their preservation on grounds of edification, and however much clerics may have enjoyed such poems unofficially, it would have been another matter to use precious parchment to preserve them.

Beowulf, although the date of its composition is probably not far removed from those of these two poems, displays quite a different tone. This is not to say that the hero does not possess the qualities of the ideal Germanic hero—Beowulf does not lack any of those mentioned by Tacitus—nor does it mean that the action is set outside the boundaries of the Germanic world. Most of it takes place in Geatland and Denmark, and frequent mention is made of other Germanic tribes and of stories from common Germanic legend. What is missing is the pure joy in battle. The poem has been tamed, and the Christian colouring has penetrated much further than the occasional mention of God to be found in *Waldere*. Allusion at this level there is in plenty; the ancestry of monsters like Grendel is attributed to Cain; the sun is called 'Heaven's candle' or 'the bright beacon of God'; the spring thaw comes when 'the Father unbinds the fetters of the pond'. Again Hrothgar's minstrel, like Cædmon, sings of the Creation to entertain the retainers in hall. These examples could be called mere decoration or attributed to a Christian interpolator. Less superficial is Beowulf's summing up of his life with its blend of the Christian and Germanic philosophies. With his dying words he claims:

> In my home I awaited what destiny had in store; I kept well what was my own. I did not look for treacherous quarrels. Nor did I swear any oaths wrongfully. For all this may I, though sick with a fatal wound, have solace, because the Lord of men has no need to charge me with the murder of my kinsfolk.   2736–45

The poem itself ends with lines in praise of Beowulf; instead of proclaiming his warlike spirit and great exploits the emphasis is laid on his mildness and gentleness, showing clearly the moderating influence of Christianity:

> So the Geatish people, the companions in the hall, mourned the
> death of their lord. They said that of all earthly kings he was the
> mildest and gentlest of men, the kindest to his people, and the most
> eager for renown.   3178–82

The Battle of Maldon, some centuries later, still has the old
heroic spirit, but there is now no doubt that the hero is a Christian hero; witness Byrhtnoth's dying prayer:

> I give you thanks, Ruler of the people, for all the benefits of this
> world. Now, gentle Lord, I have great need for you to grant my soul
> joy; allow my spirit to journey to you, Lord of the angels, travel
> with peace into your keeping.   173–9

It also has a sense of patriotism, of belonging to one's country,
that is not found in the earlier poems. There the lack of anything
in the nature of a national interest is quite noticeable, however
strong may be the loyalty between lord and retainer. Among the
primitive Germanic peoples clan and kinship were far more
prominent than the idea of nationality as such: at Maldon men of
Essex, Mercia and Northumberland are fighting for their
country and their king as well as for their lord. England has
come of age.

'BEOWULF'

We have so far established that *Beowulf* is a poem embodying
the old Germanic heroic virtues, presented through the mediating
influence of Christianity. But this in itself is no compelling reason
for reading the poem as literature. There are indeed many other
reasons for using the poem; it has even been used in evidence in
a court of law—at the inquest on the Sutton Hoo treasure, where
the descriptions of funerals were used as evidence of the intentions of those who buried the ship and its treasure. But such
archaeological and anthropological readings are irrelevant to the
question of whether *Beowulf* has any literary value.

We have already summarised the main story at the beginning
of this chapter, and like all such summaries it is somewhat bald
and unconvincing. But we are in good company: Aristotle
summarised the *Odyssey* even more briefly:

> A man is away from home for many years; he is jealously watched by Poseidon and loses all his companions. Meanwhile suitors are living in his house, wasting his possessions and plotting against his son. He arrives, tempest-tossed, makes himself known to certain people, and having attacked his enemies, destroys them while preserving himself. This is the kernel of the plot; the rest is episode.
>
> POETICS XVIII, 5

Beowulf too has episodes and digressions from the main story. In them come references to the stories of other heroes: Sigemund the dragon slayer, who appears in Norse legend as Sigurd, and in Wagner's *Ring* as Siegfried: Finn and Hengest whom we have already mentioned: Ingeld, and the attempt to heal a feud by marriage: the unpleasant character of the queen of Offa, the king of the Angles, and ancestor of Offa of Mercia. The original audience knew these stories and could recognise other more casual references, just as well as they already knew the story of Beowulf; such stories were part of their common heritage. Our poet had no need to spell them out in detail for his audience to catch the parallels; they would not lose the ironies of many of them. For those who can follow the thread the poem in fact displays considerable artistic powers of organisation which are not apparent in a summary, and the episodes and digressions are skilfully used to illustrate and intensify the plot.

The three fights with monsters which are the core of the story form a progression of increasing difficulty. In the first, Beowulf uses his immense strength to kill Grendel bare-handed; in the fight with Grendel's mother he has to resort to sword and armour, and even then the outcome is touch and go. His motives have changed also; they are now more worldly; he is avenging the death of Æschere with the promise of a reward. Rather than disinterestedly trying to destroy evil, he is now engaged in a feud demanded by the Germanic conception of honour. His third fight brings his death, though he kills the dragon. His motives and attitude are more worldly again. He is, it is true, trying to destroy the oppressor of his people, but all the same he dies rejoicing in the treasure he has won, little knowing that ironically because of a curse it is useless to anyone:

> I utter my thanks to the ruler of all things, the King of Glory, the eternal Lord, for these treasures which I look upon here, in that I have been able to gain such things for my people before I die.
>
> 2794-8

The poet does not represent this progression as any decline of spiritual virtues in the hero, but rather as a rise in worldly glory, never in itself decried. Love of honour and wealth is by no means out of place in the poem, for without it in the first place there could be no tragedy in the fact of its transience.

The cohesion of the poem is further helped by the interweaving of contrasts and parallels which run as an ironic commentary on people and events. Offa's wicked queen is contrasted with the good Freawaru, Hrothgar's daughter and Ingeld's bride; the proud and selfish Heremod highlights by contrast Beowulf's ideal qualities. After the death of Grendel's mother, the minstrel sings appropriately enough of the most famous monster-killer in Northern legend, of Sigemund who slew the dragon Fafnir, thus foreshadowing, to us who know the story, Beowulf's final fight. So too does the tragic fate of Queen Hildeburgh in the story of Finn reflect the fate predicted for Wealtheow and her family.

The first part of the poem tells of the hero's youth and rise to fame and success; its tone is chiefly heroic, and the digressions tell of heroic and legendary exploits. And this is proper; the hero is a strong and vigorous young man accomplishing heroic deeds. All the same this part also has hints of future darkness and decline, sown even early on at the peak of Danish success, that prepare us for the treachery and disaster that is to come. Hrothgar's hall, Heorot:

> towered up high and wide-gabled. It awaited the rising of battle and hateful fire. It was not yet near the time when the feud between son and father-in-law should spring up because of deadly hatred.
>
> 81-85

Again when it was damaged in Beowulf's fight with Grendel the Danes were amazed; they had thought that no man could harm it except by fire, an ironic remark not lost on those who know its final fate to be burnt down when the marriage of Freawaru to

The first leaf of Alfred's Pastoral Care.

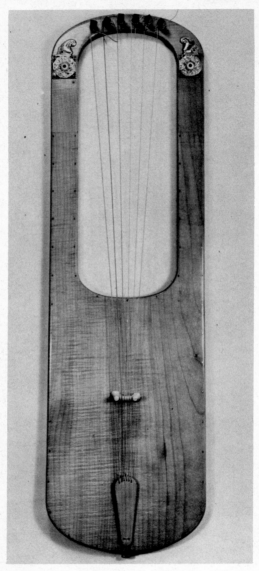

A modern reconstruction of the Sutton Hoo harp.

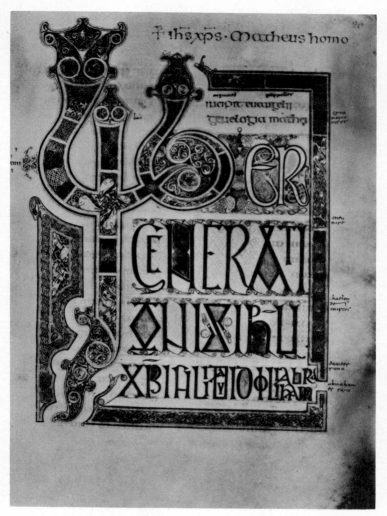

The beginning of St. Matthew's Gospel in the Vulgate manuscript of the Gospels, written and illuminated at Lindisfarne, Northumbria, about A.D. 698.

A leaf from Beowulf, the epic poem, written in Old English, about A.D. 1009

Ingeld has failed to stop the feud. The audience also knew that Hrothulf, Hrothgar's nephew, was to kill his cousin, Hrothgar's son, even though at the time of the action of *Beowulf*:

> The two noble men, nephew and uncle were seated; there was still
> peace between them; each was loyal to the other.   1163–5

But these words, and Wealtheow's pleas to Beowulf to protect her sons if any misfortune should befall them, come too soon after the Finn episode and the story of Hildeburgh for their significance to escape.

The subject of the second part of the poem is Beowulf's last fight in his old age; appropriately enough the tone is less heroic and more autumnal or elegiac. The digressions, which in the earlier part told of heroic and legendary exploits, are now mostly concerned with history, in part to make clear the events that made Beowulf king, but chiefly to show the decline of the Geatish dynasty, just as Beowulf himself has to die. The first part hinted of what was to come; the second remembers what has passed. The courageous action of Wiglaf in defending his master is like that of the young, brave and enthusiastic Beowulf, loyal to Hygelac and Hrothgar. And the poem closes, as it opened, with a splendid funeral. Then it was Scyld's, the founder of the Danish dynasty; now it is Beowulf's own, the last of the Geatish kings.

The poem, then, is well constructed for those who have the background knowledge to follow the links. We have been able to give only a few hints, and the modern reader must rely on the notes of scholars for the information that the original audience would have had at its fingertips. But construction is not enough to explain its popularity. *Beowulf* may have come down to us in a single manuscript, but if all the echoes that have been detected in other Old English poems are in fact conscious echoes then copies must have once been very much more numerous.

Like many other poems, this one has no title in the manuscript; *Beowulf* is a comparatively recent title for it. But it is the most fitting title for a poem which recounts the most significant events in the life of a hero: how he first won fame and later met his end, fighting against more than human adversaries. It is these adversaries, the monsters and the dragon, which give the poem its special power—and it must have some power to have survived at all. Some have called this power the quality of myth, but what they mean by 'myth' is something far removed from what the anthropologist or the anthropologically minded understand by it. 'True myth', according to Robert Graves, 'may be defined as the reduction to narrative shorthand of ritual mime performed on public festivals.' Nor is it the expression of a primitive subconscious of the Jungians. Some commentators have connected Beowulf with a corn god and with fertility myths, but, while such a comparison may be of interest to anthropologists, this conjecture is not really helpful as an explanation of the poem as a poem.

Still the fact remains that some stories catch the imagination, and have the power to move in whatever form they are told. Housman once said that great poetry was that which made his bristles stand on end if it came into his mind while shaving—a test whose application is rather limited—but he was probably talking about a similar sort of quality which is more easily recognised than defined. The story of Orpheus has got it; every age has told this story for itself, in film and operetta as well as word, without destroying its power to move. From Northern mythology comes the death of Balder or the Doom of the Gods itself, for unlike the Olympian gods, who at times seem almost to be larking about in a celestial Greyfriars, the Northern gods are subject to time, and are doomed to die gloriously in the final battle. *Beowulf*, too, has something of this quality, but because the whole question is so subjective we must leave each reader to decide how and how much for himself.

It is also difficult to discuss the qualities of the verse itself; here the problem is the amount of knowledge and experience needed for the full appreciation of every nuance, and at this we can only hint. Nevertheless the verse is important. *Beowulf* has a balanced structure; we see the hero in youth and old age; his rise and fall, for all men are mortal. Balance also is the basis of Old English metre with its line of two halves of equivalent weight linked by alliteration.

One facet of the verbal skill of the poet can be seen in the treatment of the hero and his opponents. We are never actually told what Beowulf himself looks like, yet we are impressed by his powerful bearing and stature which enabled a coastguard instantly to pick him out as leader of the Geats, by his heroism, by his skill at oratory, and his wisdom. It is then rather a shock to realise that we know the man without knowing what he looks like and that what we do know about him has only come in hints. The same is true of Grendel and his mother; these monsters are never described, and with more reason, for they become more terrible, not less, when they are only defined by hints. The lack of physical detail allows more scope to the imagination. Sometimes Grendel is presented as a descendant of Cain, at others he is like a tall man, at others again a deadly inhabitant of Hell; always we are conscious of the terror of his presence in passages like these:

The terrible spirit was called Grendel, the notorious wanderer of the wasteland. He held command of the marshes, of the fenland and of the fastness. The wretched creature dwelt for a while in the land of monsters after the Creator had condemned him.   102–6

The savage and greedy creature of destruction was ready immediately, fierce and furious.   120–22

The fiend, the dark shadow of death, was persecuting the retainers, old and young; he lay in wait and plotted. In the endless darkness he held the misty moors. No man knew where such demons of hell go in their wanderings.   159–63

Then came Grendel journeying from the moors over the misty slopes; he carried God's anger with him.   710–11

That such absence of description is deliberate we can best show by reference to another passage which skilfully portrays the landscape. It is not that the poet was incapable of close description, but that close description was inappropriate. Given the right context he can describe and do so very well, aided by a use of poetic compounds which pack a lot of meaning into a little space:

The mysterious evil spirits live in a hidden land with wolf-infested hillsides, windswept cliffs, dangerous paths through the fens, where a mountain stream flows down under the mists of the headland, a flood under the earth. It is not many miles from here that the lake stands, over which hangs a grove of frost-covered trees. The deeply-rooted forest overshadows the water. Every night a fearful wonder may be seen there: the water on fire. There lives none of the sons of men who is wise enough to know its bottom. Although the heath-stalker, the sturdy-horned hart, harassed by hounds, makes for the forest, chased from afar, he would rather forfeit his life on its bank than plunge in to save himself. It is no safe place. From the lake turbulent waves rise up darkly towards the clouds when the wind stirs up a fearful storm, until the sky grows gloomy and the heavens weep.   1357-76

Despite the beauty and vividness of this description, which is not entirely lost in the translation, a poem of three thousand lines would be very dull if it were filled with nothing but heroic speeches and terrifying landscapes. But it never falls into monotony; apart from the numerous digressions and shifts in the narrative, the style and tone changes, so that within the poem are seen some of the best heroic, elegiac and homiletic passages in the whole of Old English literature.

'THE BATTLE OF MALDON'

The Battle of Maldon, a 10th-century poem, is also skilfully handled in a way that makes it one of the best expressions of the heroic spirit; it stands out in a more favourable light than the comparable historical poems in the *Chronicle*. We will therefore take it as an example of them all. Although the beginning and end have been damaged, in all probability little has been lost, certainly not enough to affect our judgment of the poem. Its subject, as we have already said, is the minor battle which took place outside Maldon between Viking invaders and the inhabitants of Essex. The English force is lead by the earl Byrhtnoth, who is the very embodiment of the heroic code, and the poem tells from an English point of view of his death and the subsequent Danish victory.

Although the poem commemorates an historic event, the poet was far less interested in giving a well-documented account of what happened than in conveying the courage and loyalty of the English army. We never hear the names of the Viking leaders, but what seems like every last detail of Byrhtnoth's speeches to his men is lovingly given. The battle is presented as a series of individual combats and speeches, each one impressing on us more firmly the heroic qualities of the English, so that even if we can see only an outline of the action we know what it felt like to fight beside the River Blackwater that day.

The poem falls naturally into two parts. The first is chiefly concerned with Byrhtnoth and his actions as leader, and ends with his death after his generous and quixotic gesture to the Vikings. In this he seems more like the archetypal English sportsman, whose sporting gestures are exploited by a team of professionals playing to win. But this is only a passing thought; when the Viking messenger charges him to surrender, the courage of his reply creates an expectant tension, since throughout the poem words are soon made good by deeds. The second part begins at the desertion of Offa's sons, a piece of cowardice which highlights even more clearly the bravery of the warriors who remain to fight on by the body of their fallen lord. One by one the warriors are reduced, their valour and individuality brought down in death as they vow to fight for as long as they can hold their weapons. Even the Northumbrian hostage shares the courage of the rest:

> He was the son of Ecglaf, of the brave Northumbrian race; his name was Æscferth. He never drew back from the fray, but often shot forth his arrows. Sometimes he pierced a shield with his dart, sometimes he struck a soldier. Almost every moment he dealt out an injury for as long as he could wield his weapons.   266–72

But, of course, all is in vain; they are fighting a lost battle while an old warrior, Byrhtwold, speaks their epitaph:

> Our spirit will be the braver, heart the more valiant, and courage the greater as our strength grows less. Here lies our lord, a good man cut down in the dust. May he mourn for ever who now thinks of

turning from this sword play. I am old in years; I will not go, but
intend to lie beside my lord, the most beloved of men.   312–19

Here is the epitome of the heroic spirit of which we have said so much; this statement of it gains from its setting in a poem written in a simpler and more austere style than that of *Beowulf*. It has few of the noun compounds so common elsewhere to enhance the texture of the poetry. Here the poetic value lies in the contrast between the grey landscape and the restrained descriptions of the warriors on the one hand, and the sublimity of spirit and the bravery of their words and actions on the other. Its lack of adornment means that the verse has not the richness of some of the earlier heroic poems, but as an expression of man's indomitable spirit it has few rivals in the whole of Germanic heroic literature.

6

Religious and Elegiac Poetry

Most of the poems that we are discussing are anonymous; scarcely ever do we discover even the names of the men who wrote them, and certainly nothing of their lives and personalities. The one exception happens to be the poet of the earliest extant verse, and the originator of a definite school of religious verse-writing. He is Cædmon whom we have already met receiving the gift of poetry at Whitby under the abbess Hilda somewhere between 658 and 680. His new gift was soon put to practical use:

> Then they expounded to him a passage of sacred history or doctrine, and told him, if he could, to turn it into poetry. He undertook the task and went away; in the morning he returned and recited what he had been given in excellent verse. . . .
>
> He turned everything that he could learn by ear into the pleasantest verse by memorising it and ruminating on it, and it sounded so sweet that his own teachers became his audience. He sang of the Creation of the world, the beginning of the human race, the whole story of Genesis, of the Exodus of the Israelites from Egypt and their entry into the promised land. He also composed many other stories from the sacred scriptures: about Our Lord's incarnation, passion, resurrection and ascension to Heaven; about the coming of the Holy Spirit, and the teachings of the Apostles. He made many songs, too, about the terror of the judgement that is to come, and the horror of the pains of Hell, and the joys of the Kingdom of Heaven.   Bede HIST. ECCL. IV. xxiv

On the evidence of this account of the type of poetry which Cædmon composed orally and had written down for him by the literate clergy, scholars used to believe that the biblical paraphrases in the 10th-century Junius manuscript were Cædmon's work. Junius himself ascribed them to him when he published the contents of the manuscript in Amsterdam in 1655. But in the original they have neither titles nor any indication of authorship; they are now known after their subject matter as *Genesis*, *Exodus*, *Daniel*, and *Christ and Satan*, this last being not one but a group of three poems. The discrepancies in tone, vocabulary and style of the poems, and the small chance of so much of Cædmon's work having survived when so many other clerics must have written religious poetry, give the theory of Cædmon's authorship very little weight, and we are left with knowing something of the poet but next to nothing of his work.

It is often thought that these biblical poems are the most tedious of all Old English poetry, providing nothing but line after line of close and unimaginative paraphrase of the Bible. But 'most tedious' is a relative not an absolute statement, and to dismiss these poems is to misunderstand their purpose. The poet's intentions, whoever he was, was not so much to write artful poetry as to discover an attractive way of telling stories from the scriptures. Even though none of it can rival *Beowulf* for careful construction and sheer beauty of poetry, there is much of interest in this verse.

Genesis, the first poem in the manuscript, presents an account of the incidents in the first book of the Old Testament as far as the sacrifice of Isaac. For the most part it is a rather unexceptional poem. Lines such as:

> The first born of Cain's sons was called Enoch. With his kinsmen
> he began to build a fortified city, which was the first of those walled
> strongholds that sword-girt men established beneath the heavens.
> And in this place his sons were born, the offspring of his wife in that
> city. The eldest was called Irad, the son of Enoch. Afterwards he
> begat children and the progeny and kinsmen of Cain increased.
> Mahalalel came after Irad and took his father's place as guardian of
> the property until he died. . . . 1055–68

certainly do not read like great poetry, but then neither does much of the King James's version of the Old Testament read like literature. Historical summary does not make promising material for poetry. But once or twice the poet draws away from his model and lets his imagination take over; his version of the story of Sodom and Gomorrah draws on echoes of earlier Germanic diction and on his own imagination to produce a passage of striking originality:

> Many a pale frightened woman must go trembling into a stranger's embrace. The protectors of women and treasures have fallen, sick with wounds. . . .
>
> For the last twelve winters they were obliged to pay tax and tribute to the men from the North, until the people would no longer support the prince of the Elamites with the public treasure, and rebelled against him. Then hostile armies, intent on slaughter, came together. The sound of javelins rang out. The dark bird with dewy feathers sang amid the spear shafts in the hope of carrion. The armed warriors made haste with proud spirit in powerful troops until the people had assembled an army from North and South. 1169–89

and later:

> The three brothers very speedily soothed his anxiety by their speech, valiant men with brave words, and made a pledge to Abraham that they would avenge his wrong on his enemies with him or fall in battle. 2033–8

Passages like these share not only the diction, imagery and codes of behaviour but also the swiftness of action of a poem like *The Battle of Maldon*. Here we have Christian themes mediated through pagan forms, a reversal of the position in the heroic poems which we noted earlier. These extracts certainly do not look as if they have been taken from a literal rendering of the story of Genesis. The clergy's love of tales of ancient heroes and brave deeds, which is attested by Alcuin's rebuke to the Lindisfarne monks, must have been greatly satisfied by these biblical poems. We cannot be certain whether their poets employed a Germanic flavouring to attract listeners, or whether the old poetic diction was so firmly rooted that they would have found difficulty in writing in any other way. On balance the first is the

F

more likely. After all we do much the same thing with some modern translations of the Bible which employ modern locutions in an attempt to attract modern readers. But the powerful and dramatic qualities of these passages from the paraphrases also suggest that this was perhaps the natural poetic idiom for a poet to adopt when his imagination was given free play.

In the middle of this Genesis poem is an extract from another, obviously by another poet, for its style is far superior. How they came together is unknown now, but since they are together they need to be distinguished for the purposes of reference. Thus the insert is known as *Genesis B* to distinguish it from *Genesis A*, the poem we have been discussing so far. *Genesis B* deals with the rebellion of Satan and his angels and with the fall of man. The poet differs from the writer of *Genesis A* in that he appears to have composed his poem with the Bible shut. He allows his imagination freer play, and presents a forceful, vivid picture of the fall of man in which the vigour and spirit of Satan and the weakness and pathos of Eve are prominent. The proud, rebellious Satan indeed recalls Milton's treatment of the same theme seven centuries later:

> 'Why should I labour?' he said. 'I need no master. My hands are able to accomplish very many wonders. I have great power to form a better throne in Heaven. Why must I wait upon His favour? I can be God as well as He. Resolute comrades, brave warriors who will not desert me in the fight, stand about me. These valiant heroes have chosen me as their leader.'   B 278–86

This lacks the sophisticated rhetoric of Milton's anti-hero, but these words could almost have been spoken by the Satan of *Paradise Lost* who thus spits out his defiance:

> What though the field be lost?
> All is not lost; th' unconquerable Will,
> And study of revenge, immortal hate,
> And courage never to submit or yeild:
> And what is else not to be overcome?
> That Glory never shall his wrauth or might
> Extort from mee. To bow and sue for grace

With suppliant knee, and deifie his power
Who from the terrour of this Arm so late
Doubted his Empire; that were low indeed,
That were an ignominy and shame beneath
This downfall; since by Fate the strength of Gods
And this Empyreal substance cannot fail,
Since through experience of this great event
In Arms not worse, in foresight much advanc't,
We may with more successful hope resolve
To wage by force or guile eternal Warr,
Irreconcileable to our grand Foe,
Who now triumphs, and in th' excess of joy
Sole reigning holds the Tyranny of Heav'n.

P.L. I, 105–24

But the resemblance ends here. The Old English poem has none of Milton's artistry, yet the verse does have a vigour and life that make it stand out from *Genesis A*. The poet also digresses from the rather arid paraphrase in his presentation of Eve, which displays a degree of human interest unusual in Old English poetry. He sympathises with her for falling into temptation, and blames it on the weakness of her sex. Satan's insinuations and suggestions are carefully explained so that the fall is seen to result from an error of human judgement, and the expulsion from Eden to be an object of justifiable pathos:

My friend Adam [Eve says], you may blame me for it with your words; but you cannot grieve more bitterly in your mind than I do in my heart. *B 824–6*

Exodus, the third of these paraphrases, draws most heavily on the poet's Germanic inheritance. It concentrates mainly on the Exodus itself, the coming out of the land of Egypt, the crossing of the Red Sea, and above all on the battle between the Egyptians and the Israelites. Its opening recalls the opening lines of *Beowulf*:

Lo! We have heard far and wide throughout the world how the judgements of Moses, the wondrous spoken laws, announce to warriors, to the generations of men, the reward of heavenly life to each of the blessed after death, an everlasting gain for every soul. *1–7*

And the poem goes on to employ to full effect the beasts of battle, dread harbingers of disaster, familiar from their wide use in the secular poetry. As in *Genesis B* what merit the poem has lies in the energy, swift movement and cumulative power of the Germanic diction. The poet uses an almost cinematic technique, shifting the scene back and forth from one camp to the other, pointing out the contrasting feelings in the two armies and heightening the tension before the approaching battle. This energy is also to be found in the speeches with which Moses encourages his followers, and in the vivid descriptions of the disaster which befell the Egyptians in the Red Sea:

> The people were terrified; terror of the flood gripped their wretched spirits; the ocean threatened death. The mountainous waves were spattered with blood. The sea spewed out gore. There was uproar on the waves; the water was full of weapons; a deadly mist rose up.
>
> 447–51

But once the occasion for such treatment is past, the energy is dissipated, and the remainder of the poem, including a digression about Noah and another about Abraham, is only mediocre.

Despite our attempts to point out some of the value of these biblical poems, many readers may still prefer to brush them aside as uninteresting. But before they condemn them outright, the critics should note a final argument in their favour. Nowadays the Bible stories are well known to us. We have listened to tales such as are told in the Junius manuscript from our kindergarten days, if not from our cradles. So our reading of these paraphrases tends to focus on what is original in them. The Anglo-Saxon audience was in quite a different position. The English Bible was not part of their cultural background in the same way that it is ours. They were not as familiar with the stories, and would appreciate them in much the same way as we did when they aroused our curiosity and wonder as children. They are, in fact, a species of missionary literature, and as such will certainly stand comparison with modern examples, besides being for historians and theologians a source of insight into the Anglo-Saxons' attitude to the Bible stories and their methods of presenting them.

One part of the Junius manuscript which is not solely concerned with the biblical narrative is that containing the three poems collectively called *Christ and Satan*, a modern title, remember. This part is written in a different hand and was added to the manuscript perhaps a century later. It recounts the fall of the angels, the harrowing of Hell and the temptation in the wilderness. But where one might have expected a more lively treatment the poem often has a homiletic ring: we are constantly exhorted to serve God and reject Satan:

> The Son of Glory has his throne amid the heavens. By his healing power he leads us there to the light, where we may sit with the Lord with the angels on high and enjoy that same radiance where his sacred company now dwell, and live in bliss. In this place the blessedness of glory is brilliantly displayed. Let us be mindful to eagerly serve and please Christ the Saviour.   586–95

CYNEWULF AND HIS SCHOOL

This didacticism is even more marked in another group of religious poems. Whereas the earlier biblical poetry is little more than a paraphrase of the Old Testament permeated by the old heroic traditions, these poems are marked by a didacticism allied to far more sophisticated thought and language. We know the name of the author of some of them, for four of the poems, *Elene*, *Juliana*, *The Fates of the Apostles*, and *Christ II*, contain the name Cynewulf in acrostic form—a testimony to the Anglo-Saxon fondness for riddles. But his name is the only sure fact about him; everything else must be left to conjecture. From the subject-matter of the poems and his knowledge of Latin sources it is almost certain that he was a cleric; from a study of his language it seems likely that he was an Anglian writing in the first half of the 9th century. It is true that *Elene* has what looks like an autobiographical passage. In it Cynewulf says that he was an old man steeped in sin until by divine inspiration he was given the gift of song. But such humble protestations of the author's sinfulness, and the ascription of his skill to divine intervention, are commonplaces, and therefore need not be given much credit.

The manuscripts which contain these four signed poems have a number of other poems with similar subject-matter and style. For convenience of description they are often called Cynewulfian, but it is safer to assume, as with the group of Cædmon poems, that they are the work of more than one author. There are seven of them: *Andreas*, *Guthlac A* and *Guthlac B*, *Christ I* and *III*, *The Phoenix* and *The Dream of the Rood*; the majority of them deal with the lives of saints, their courageous and miraculous deeds, and their heroic and agonising deaths.

What may seem surprising is that two of them are about women. In the heroic poetry women have only a passive role to play. They appear, but they are completely powerless creatures unable in any way to alter the designs of the dominant male. In *Beowulf*, for instance, Freawaru is given in marriage to Ingeld as a political pawn in a vain attempt to heal a feud, but in no time at all battle is raging again; Wealtheow is an impressive and elegant queen who plays little part in the narrative except to minister to the men; Hildeburgh weeps helplessly as her husband, brother and son lose their lives in acts of revenge. In a similar way in the elegiac verse, the *Wife's Lament* (see below) is the lament of a woman suffering separation from her loved one, whilst absolutely powerless to do anything about it.

Thus these poems come as something of a surprise until we realise that saints are not chosen by their sex, and that, aided by the veneration given to the Virgin Mary, the position of women in the Church and religious life has in general been favourable. But for all that, Cynewulf's *Juliana* holds little to attract the modern reader. It follows the pattern of many medieval saints' lives, telling of the young girl's struggles to preserve her virginity and faith amidst numerous threats, temptations and tortures. On these the poet dwells at harrowing length. She is stretched out naked, and scourged; she is hung up by the hair for six hours; she is tortured by fire on a wheel set with swords; she is thrown into boiling oil. These ordeals are made even more terrible because it is her father who sends her to them, but in not a single one of them does she let out so much as a whimper of pain. The poem shows no artistic merits, and her long discourse with the devil who visits her in prison is pretty dull despite much of its colourful language:

> I shall suffer and endure all things at your judgement, lay bare the dark evil which I have long contrived. Often I have taken away sight, blinded countless men with evil thoughts; covered the light of the eye with a veil of mist and dark showers from my poisonous breath. With wicked snares I have destroyed the feet of some; others I sent into the grip of the fire, so that their traces were no longer seen.
>
> 465–74

But it has its points; it is the type of verse which if Aldhelm had sung it from his bridge would have attracted his people to church by its fast-moving succession of horrific events, its picture of a beautiful maiden beset by wicked men and fearful tortures.

Elene is quite different in subject, but intended to be equally popular. It treats of the search for the cross on which Christ was crucified, a particularly interesting topic to the Anglo-Saxon audience since the Veneration of the Cross began to play an important part in church services in the 8th century. The more adventurous nature of the story allows the old heroic style to be used to great advantage, and the poem contains many vivid descriptions, such as that of St. Helena's sea voyage to Jerusalem:

> Then they let the high ships drive foaming over the ocean. Often over the turbulent water the sides of the ship took the buffeting of the waves; the sea resounded. . . . Then anyone who watched the journey would have seen the boat breaking over the sea, speeding on under swelling sails, the sea horse playing, the wave-floater journeying on.
>
> 237–46

Besides description there are fast-moving, dramatic speeches:

> Why! In your stupidity you fiercely cast aside all wisdom, when you reproached the one who through his wondrous strength intended to protect you from damnation, from burning torment, from captivity. You spat filth on the face of him who by his sacred spittle restored the light of your eyes and cured your blindness and saved you from unclean evil spirits.
>
> 293–302

The result is a highly-coloured poem in which the scene is continually shifting and the tone is dramatically varied.

All the saints' lives display an attraction towards the remote and fantastic; this is most evident in *Andreas*, a poem whose author and provenance are unknown. It derives from the apocryphal *Acts of SS Matthew and Andrew*. It has also often been pointed out that there are many signs throughout the poem that the author was greatly influenced by *Beowulf* and borrowed a great deal whether relevant or not. Numerous phrases recall *Beowulf* and the resemblance extends to whole episodes such as Andrew's journey by ship with a band of companions to Mermedonia to combat man-eating beasts, just as Beowulf sailed to Denmark to destroy the monsters. This might be a sign that even in these early times *Beowulf* was acclaimed as a great poem; the author of *Andreas* used these borrowings to add weight and authority to his poem in much the same way as Milton filled *Paradise Lost* with reminiscences of Virgil. But, this question of borrowing apart, we have in *Andreas* a poem of adventure and excitement laced with a good deal of didacticism. Andrew sets off across treacherous seas to rescue his fellow-apostle, Matthew, from the cannibal Mermedonians, and after many torments succeeds, and ends by converting them all. There are secret potions, countless miracles, a flood and many narrow escapes, and while not being as good a job as *Beowulf* it has many merits of its own. It has been thoughtfully constructed with the Saint's calm and patience accentuated by contrast with the stormy seas in the first half, and with the ragings of the Mermedonians and devils in the second; the conversion of the Mermedonians by the water flowing from the pillar at the end of the poem mirrors Andrew's words at the beginning about God's command to the image in the temple to convert the Jews.

There are several notable passages which we might have chosen as illustrations, and we have taken two, one of which is a description of pain and torture far more realistic than those in *Juliana*:

> My limbs are strained apart; my bones painfully broken, my body blood-stained; the gory gashes of my wounds gush forth. . . .
>
> Now my tendons are torn; my blood has flowed out, my hair

is scattered abroad, my locks upon the land. Far dearer to me is
death than this tortured life.   1404–7; 1425–8

The description of the wintry countryside, one of the things that
Old English poetry is good at, mirrors the atmosphere of the
prison cell and intensifies the mood of misery, but for our second
passage we have taken a storm from Andrew's sea voyage;

> Then the whale-ocean began to be stirred and aroused. Whales
> leaped, darted through the sea, and the grey sea-mew circled
> round, hungry for carrion. The candle of the sky grew dark;
> the winds rose; the waves crashed together; the sea was in uproar;
> the rigging groaned and the sheets were drenched.   369–75

Again and again in all these poems the poet turns to describe
the sea, even when there is no occasion for such descriptions in
his sources. (In *Christ II* the sea is an image of human life and
God guiding man to safety.) This love of the sea, suggested by
the beauty and force of many of these passages, gives weight to
any inference that these poems even if not all by Cynewulf
himself are the product of a local tradition of verse-writing,
perhaps centred on a coastal monastery.

Reading these Old English saints' stories, we inevitably notice
other characteristics that they share. One must search in vain for
realism in the story; they are full of sensational miracles and
tortures. Andrew causes a great flood to demonstrate the existence
of God to the pagans; Juliana is saved from her torments by the
intervention of an angel. But this stress on miracles and the
supernatural has an important part to play by providing a setting
in which the saints' saintliness may shine forth. To show heroic
resistance to temptation and torture one must have more than
ordinary temptations and tortures to be resisted; 'an everyday
story of country folk' would not serve. We are, or should be, far
more impressed when we hear of the terrible torture which these
saints could endure, or read the firm arguments with which they
could set forth their faith and crush the terrifying devils. Equally
well the miracles demonstrate in concrete fashion how God can
intervene for those who love Him. These stories are not history.
The poets' purpose was to praise the heroes of God, and to set

them up as examples for our edification. And if in doing so the moral is set in a pleasing and entertaining form, tales of the supernatural and sensational fulfil the desire for the marvellous and exciting which has been a feature of popular literature throughout the ages.

The other poems in this group are more lyrical than narrative; they include one that stands out supreme above all the other religious poetry as an expression of a deeply-felt personal faith. This is the *Dream of the Rood*, or dream about the Cross. Some lines of an older version are carved in runes on the 8th-century stone cross at Ruthwell in Dumfriesshire; two lines survive on the 10th-century Brussels cross; while the complete poem is found only in one late 10th-century manuscript, the Vercelli Book. The appearance of quotations on two such devotional works of art is strong evidence for its significance to its Anglo-Saxon audience. It also differs from the other religious poems which we have been discussing so far, and whose Latin originals are never hard to find, in that its source is obscure, though some have observed a resemblance to Latin hymns such as the *Vexilla Regis* of Venantius Fortunatus (*c.*530–?609), where Christ is presented in his Passion as both victorious king and suffering man. But while the liturgy could have been a source of inspiration for this poet as for many others, the connexion is only conjectural. Moreover it cannot explain the form of the poem. While there are other accounts of dreams—Bede's story of Cædmon, for instance—it is not until several centuries later that the dream/allegory motif becomes frequent as the articulating structure of a poem. It seems surprising to find an example so carefully developed in the 8th century.

There are three parts to the poem. In the first the narrator tells how in a dream he saw a brightly shining cross adorned with gold and jewels and venerated by angels; yet beneath the splendour he could see the bare wood, stained with blood. In the next part the cross itself speaks. With simplicity it recounts that it was once a tree in the forest, cut down to make a cross for Christ. It goes on to give an account of the Passion and burial, and ends with advice to the dreamer to encourage the Veneration of the

Cross. In the third part the dreamer no longer feels sorrow for his sins, but hope in the triumph of Christ on the Cross and longs to leave this world and attain the joys of heaven.

The *Dream* is different from the other, more crudely constructed poems which we have been discussing so far. Beneath its austere and compact style there lies a web of subtleties and paradoxes which point to a sophistication remarkable for such an early period. There is a skilfully preserved balance and duality maintained throughout the poem. This balance reflects the Church's view of the co-existence of the two aspects of Christ in his crucifixion, the human and the divine. It can be seen in the presentation in the poem of Christ as both the victorious hero climbing willingly on to the cross, and as the man suffering at the hands of wicked men, a paradox reinforced many times throughout the poem: 'I saw the God of Hosts cruelly stretched out,' 'then they laid him down with weary limbs, stood by his head, and looked on the Lord of Heaven.' But we can also see it in the alternation between the cross as a radiant bejewelled sign and as bare blood-stained wood in its description as first a tree and then the bearer of Christ's sufferings. In the account of the Passion it bears the gashes of the nails and the taunts of the persecutors; yet when Christ is seen as a Germanic hero boldly climbing on to the cross, then the cross becomes the retainer boldly serving his lord. And this image of the Germanic hero is continued in the description of the burial, when the 'warriors', his disciples, take him down from the cross and look on their 'triumphant lord', and as at Beowulf's funeral sing a dirge round their master's tomb. A further contrast is that between the sin-stained dreamer and the splendid cross. 'The cross of victory was wondrous, and I stained with sin, afflicted with wrong.' 'I was greatly troubled with sorrows; I was afraid because of the beautiful vision.' Contrasts such as these provide much of the motivation of the final portion, and it is the words of the sinner which give the poem much of its sincerity and deep feeling. But despite the constant shifts of perspective demanded by the web of balanced paradox, the whole poem is consistently well managed; never does it become clumsy or confused.

The Passion itself is the most moving and beautifully written in early literature. Its style is unadorned, and reaches a climax in the final simple and poignant line: 'Crist wæs on rode.'

> I was raised up as a cross; I supported the great King, the Lord of Heaven; I dared not bow. They pierced me through with dark nails; the scars are plain to see on me, open wounds of malice. I dared not harm any of them. They reviled us both together. I was completely drenched in blood, shed from the man's side after he had given up his spirit. I have suffered many harsh trials on the hill. I saw the Lord of Hosts cruelly stretched out. Darkness had covered the Lord's body, the bright radiance with clouds; shadows went forth, dark under the clouds. All creation wept, lamented the fall of the King. Christ was on the cross.   44–56

The last section falls short of the high standard set at the beginning. Yet though it cannot match such passages as the Passion and the vision of the cross, it nevertheless does nothing to hinder the cohesion of the poem, and maintains the depth of feeling which pervades the earlier part, despite a more homiletic tone. The dreamer who at first was troubled by his sins and was awe-struck by the glory of the vision, in the end reflects the triumph of Christ on the cross in a mood of exaltation, and longs to flee the world and enjoy God's glory. Thus the poem finally proclaims the saving powers of the cross.

THE ELEGIES

In the last speech of the dreamer there are a number of sentiments expressed which are to be seen in other poems: solitude, loss of friends, desire to leave the transient joys of this world. These feelings are found throughout Old English poetry, but more especially in the group of poems known as elegies. These poems include *The Ruin, The Wanderer, The Seafarer, Deor, The Wife's Lament, Wulf and Eadwacer*, and *The Husband's Message*. There are also two passages in *Beowulf* which are elegiac in tone and style. Many critics have discouraged grouping these poems together under the common head of elegy, but they do share enough features to make it worth discussing them together, and the title of elegy can be justified.

'Elegy' for the modern reader will usually call to mind such poems as *In Memoriam*, *Lycidas* or *Adonais* in which the poet expresses his grief at the death of someone near him. But there is also another kind of elegy expressing a more universal sorrow. One of these is Gray's *Elegy Written in a Country Churchyard*, and it is elegies such as this which form the majority of the surviving ones from the Old English period. There is only one death elegy: that of the father's lament in *Beowulf*. These are therefore more likely to strike a chord with the modern reader. They are concerned with universal feelings, experienced today as they have always been—like Gray's:

> The boast of heraldry, the pomp of power,
> And all that beauty, all that wealth e'er gave,
> Awaits alike th'inevitable hour:
> The paths of Glory lead but to the grave.

The subject-matter of these Old English poems varies a great deal, from secular to Christian, from personal love-lament to general sorrow for the fate of man, but they do have certain features in common. At bottom each poem at some stage contrasts the sorrow of the present with past happiness, dwelling upon the transience of life's pleasures and the fallaciousness of its security. There are also a number of minor features which occur often enough to regard them as conventions of the Old English elegy; these include narration in the first person, the sense of isolation of the narrator who has lost all who are dear to him, and the use of weather and ruins to reinforce the feelings of decay and transitoriness. One poem, indeed, *The Ruin*, is a lament over a ruined city, probably Bath, where the decaying Roman masonry of the once great city provides a paradigm of the transience of worldly splendour cast down by fate.

The two finest and most complex elegies are *The Wanderer* and *The Seafarer*, but their complexity has led to a vast amount of discussion about their interpretation. It is almost generally considered now that each poem is complete in itself and each the work of a single poet, rather than the piecing together of pagan and Christian extracts by a variety of hands. The poems exhibit the progression of a positive train of thought, developed by means of parallels and structural detail, which would not be as likely in a patchwork. Their theme is exile, a much worse fate in those days when the protection of one's lord established one's place in society.

The Wanderer has a six-line prologue, the narrative by the solitary exile, and a six-line epilogue. The Wanderer tells of his loneliness and the loss of his lord:

> He who has had experience knows how cruel a companion sorrow is for the man who has few dear protectors.   29–31

He dreams of the happiness of the past, when he enjoyed the favour of his lord and his gifts in hall, but wakes to find only the dark waves and the sea-birds for company. Throughout the comparison between his past and present, the icy waters and the harsh weather mirror his feelings of desolation:

> So, worn out by cares, cut off from my native land and from my kinsmen, I often had to fetter my thoughts, when in years gone by the darkness of the earth covered my generous lord and I went thence in misery with wintry care over the frozen waves.   19–24

He similarly uses the image of the hall to indicate the warmth and companionship that he has lost—remember Bede's simile of the sparrow from Chapter 4. This contemplation of his own sorrow leads the Wanderer to thinking of the sadness of the world, the death of rulers, and decay of splendid buildings, and thence to the wisdom of looking beyond the transience of this world. The scope of the poem widens as he progresses into a passage lamenting in a series of rhetorical questions the passing of worldly joys:

> Where has the horse gone, where the man, where the treasure giver? Where has the banquet hall gone? Where are the joys of the feast?   92–3

and reaches a climax in the line:

> The whole structure of the earth becomes desolate.   110

At this note of utter misery the epilogue introduces the consolation of hope in God. The word *are*, 'mercy', found also in the prologue, reappears to link the end with the beginning, and to stress that the goodness of God is the only firm thing on which one can place one's trust. Thus the thought of the poem progresses in a steady advance from hopelessness, through realisation of the impermanence of earthly joys, to consolation in God.

The Seafarer can be divided into two parts, the first being a description of the sea and a desire to be away on a voyage, and the second being moralising on the transience of life. Its more abrupt transition between the two has led some scholars to think of it as either two separate poems or a dialogue between an old seaman pointing out the harshness of life at sea and a young man eager to be away. As is usual there is no indication in the manuscript to help settle the question of the poet's intention, but there is sufficient fusion of thought and material to allow *The Seafarer* to be taken as a single monologue complete in itself.

The poem's development of thought resembles that of *The Wanderer*. The Seafarer is not an exile, but nevertheless because of his trade knows the sorrows of loneliness, dark waves and freezing cold:

> There storms battered against the stony cliffs; there the tern answered icy-feathered; often the dewy-winged eagle screamed aloud. No protector was there to console the despairing mind.
>
> 23–6

As in *The Wanderer* the poet uses the external elements of cold, storm and darkness to render the internal misery more vivid. The harsh screaming of the sea birds, the howling of the wind and the storm emphasise the Seafarer's lack of companions:

> I heard nothing there except the resounding of the sea, the icy waves, and sometimes the cry of the swan.
>
> 18–19

Despite the hardships of the sea he scorns the easy life on shore and is anxious to be back. Some have understood this whole seafaring section in connection with the second half as an allegorical account of the desire to depart from life. A parallel example would be *Christ II* where Cynewulf uses a sea voyage to illustrate man's life on earth. But there is no need to take the poem as an allegory. As with the Wanderer, the Seafarer's own miseries lead his thoughts outwards to consider those of mankind in general. It is the turning away from earthly pleasure that brings the poem rather abruptly on to the wider consideration of transience and thence to trust in God. Here his thoughts throw light on his previous desire to seek the hardships of the sea:

> For this reason the praise of the living, spoken in later days, is the best posthumous fame for every man; that before he died he strove after earthly benefits, and accomplished brave deeds against the malice of enemies and the devil. 72–77

He ponders the inevitability of death and the impossibility of taking one's riches beyond the grave. So naturally he goes on to consider the power of God and ways of attaining the only lasting happiness. Although *The Seafarer* lacks the framework and the same degree of careful construction found in *The Wanderer*, it presents with the same vividness and beauty a mood of melancholy which is heightened by the continuous image of winter.

Another group of elegies have as their subject a topic which is only too rare in Old English poetry: love between men and women. It is probably not by chance that so little love poetry has survived. The steely Teutonic temperament would not have encouraged such songs, nor perhaps the Church, despite the example of the *Song of Songs*, and it was not until French influence took root after the Conquest that much love poetry was written. The whole concept of romantic love which we take for granted today began in the late 11th century amongst the Troubadours of Languedoc, and, though the excesses of 'courtly love' did not outlast the medieval period, their attitude to women is the basis of even modern love poetry. There are three of these love elegies: *Wulf and Eadwacer*, *The Wife's Lament* and *The Husband's Message*; unlike the others they draw no generalisations about man's lot here on earth, but are entirely personal. Unfortunately for us, all three of them are based on stories which are now lost, though doubtless familiar enough to the original audience. We can only guess at the thread of the stories and their setting, but still we lose little of the emotional force behind the speaker's words.

The narrator of both *The Wife's Lament* and *Wulf and Eadwacer* is a woman. The first of these, the most elegiac of the three poems is the lament of a woman separated from her husband and persecuted by her foes. She finds no consolation at the end, only a grim endurance of her grief. The poem abounds in words denoting misery, and has as well many of the elegiac conventions mentioned above; she is a 'friendless exile' with 'few dear friends'; the dwellings are in ruins, abandoned and overgrown, the weather stormy. Each brings with it a store of associations to intensify the misery. *Wulf and Eadwacer* is less straightforward, which makes it harder to understand and opens the door to several interpretations. The one most often adopted is that the narrator is separated from her lover, Wulf, by being kept on an island by Eadwacer, who is probably her husband. With *The Wife's Lament* this poem resembles the medieval *genre* known as *Frauenlied* in which women bewail their misfortunes in love. The repetition of the line 'It is not so with us' gives a haunting quality to the lament where the rain falling in response to her tears gives yet another example of the use of natural phenomena to illustrate and underline internal emotions.

The third poem, *The Husband's Message*, is too optimistic to be a true elegy; its sorrows are in the past. The separation of the lovers, so sorely lamented in the previous two poems, is about to end, and the husband writes to his wife to assure her of his faith and to tell her of the home he has prepared for her in another land. Here the exile is almost over, and sorrow is about to be replaced by joy. So much of Old English verse is wintry that the sound of the cuckoo and the promise of future pleasure come as a pleasant surprise, and make what we hope is an appropriate place to close our survey; may the promise be fulfilled if you come to explore this poetry further!

A feud drove him from his victorious people. He himself now bids me tell you joyfully to put to sea as soon as you hear the mournful cuckoo singing in the wood by the cliff's edge. Then let no man alive hinder you, keep you from your voyage. Make for the sea, the home of the sea-mew; embark on the boat so that you may come south from here over the ocean ways and find the prince where he is longing for you. THE HUSBAND'S MESSAGE 20–30

7

Epilogue: Of Books and Manuscripts

The common permanent writing material in the ancient world was papyrus—two layers of thin strips of the pith of the reed-like papyrus plant from the Nile Delta laid crosswise, dried and polished. It gave a reasonable writing surface on one side, and the supply was adequate, but it was brittle when folded and thus used normally for scrolls only. Its use was confined to Mediterranean lands. The other writing materials were vellum or parchment. Both are treated animal skins and there is little practical difference between them, though 'vellum' tends to be used for the finer product. Skins, usually of the smaller farm animals and in particular of sheep, calves or goats, are treated with lime to remove the hairs as in the first stages of making leather. But instead of being tanned they are scraped, washed and stretched out to dry before being finished with chalk and pumice to give a smooth creamy-white surface on both sides. Parchment was more expensive than papyrus, but was flexible enough to fold without cracking and had a good writing surface on both sides, thus permitting the development of the book, which is much easier to use than the papyrus roll. The supply was obviously limited by the number of animals available for slaughter each year. Paper, thin sheets of felted vegetable fibres, was discovered in China early on. One tradition ascribes its invention to one Tsai-Lun, a minister of agriculture under the emperor Ho-Ti, in AD 105, but papermaking was confined to the Far East until the Arabs sacked Samarkand in 704 and brought the art to the West. The Moors introduced it to Spain by the 11th century; there are records of paper being made in Toledo in 1085. From Spain it spread to the rest of Europe and somewhat later to England, where the first recorded papermill was erected at Stevenage in about 1490. In many ways paper is inferior to parchment, but its supply is not subject to the same limitations, which makes it cheaper and able to meet the demands of the printing press for a plentiful raw material for the mass production of books.

The specifications for an acceptable writing ink are quite exacting. The problem is to produce a fluid that makes permanent marks, not subject to fading either with age or exposure to light. It should not clog the pen or corrode it, and be stable enough not to go off too rapidly before it can be used. It should penetrate the writing surface far enough and dry rapidly enough so that the writing does not wash off or smudge, but not penetrate so far that it feathers and makes the letters run together, or dry before it leaves the pen. Before the 19th-century growth of the chemical industry with its work on artificial dyes there were two types of writing ink: carbon, such as lamp black, with gum to give adhesion, and one based on the colour-producing reaction between tannin, found especially in oak galls, and iron salts. Chinese ink was of the first type and applied with a brush (Indian drawing ink is a modern example); but the second type was commoner in the medieval West, and was used with quill pens.

Manuscripts are much the same size and shape as printed books; their purpose is the same, and what is conveniently handlable now was no less so then. The page size of an average utilitarian manuscript, of homilies say, is about 10 × 7 ins., or the size of a double page spread of this book. More splendid manuscripts were often much larger, and of course there were many smaller ones. But the unit in making a manuscript is the double leaf, folded in half to give two leaves or four pages. A number of these, usually four in the 8th to 12th centuries, are folded together to make a quire; a number of quires are sown together to make the manuscript. The scribe, then, is originally faced with a sort of dressmaking problem in reverse; instead of trying to get irregular pieces out of a rectangular length of cloth, he has to get a number of rectangular pieces of parchment (14 × 10 ins. in our average MS.) out of an irregular skin, whose quality, just to make things more awkward, varies from part to part, the underbelly being poorest. It is not all that easy to make an economical use of a skin. Try laying out pieces of paper on a natural sheep or goatskin rug, and most rugs have had the worst irregularities trimmed off. A small skin—the best quality comes from a young and therefore small animal—will probably only produce two double leaves; twenty-five small skins, and therefore twenty-five animals, will be needed to produce a manuscript of a hundred leaves. St. Francis of Assisi had the habit of picking up any stray piece of parchment, even from pagan books. He explained that it was not sacrilegious because the letters on them were capable of forming God's name; they were also too precious to waste, for parchment can be scraped clean and used again.

A scribe takes the (four) sheets which make a quire and arranges them so that hair side faces hair side and flesh side flesh side—the two sides of a sheet of parchment present a slightly different appearance. He then marks out the writing area and the position of the lines by pricking through all four sheets at a time. Each sheet is then ruled on the hair side with a pointed instrument, the quire is reassembled and folded in half with the hair side outside, and writing can begin.

Scribal practice was marked by a paucity of punctuation and an abundance of abbreviation and contraction, which both lightened the labour of writing and saved precious parchment. So, too, verse is written continuously with no account being taken of the lines. But the reader of a modern edition is shielded from all this by the labours of editors, and, having noted the large part editors have to play in the presentation of texts, there is little more that we can usefully say here, though the study of the development of scripts is a fascinating study in its own right.

These are the main physical constraints which bear on the production of manuscripts, and which make it such a serious business. To these we could also add the absence of efficient artificial light and heating which would make writing a penance in the colder and darker seasons of the year. We could also add the moral question of the purpose of writing. Alcuin pondered this in a Latin poem on a monastic scriptorium in which he recommends scribes to comport themselves with dignity and reverence in speech and bearing to befit the holiness of the books they are to copy and to aid the accurate reproduction of the text. Writing is more refined labour than cultivation of the land; it also serves the soul's welfare.

THE PRESERVATION OF MANUSCRIPTS

Until the Dissolution of the Monasteries, manuscripts remained in their monastic libraries, but they were not safe even there. By the 13th or 14th century they were generally considered worthless, for there were few except those with a specially cultivated antiquarian taste who could read them. But the real disaster was the Dissolution itself. In the four years 1536 to 1539 monasteries throughout the country were sequestrated by the Crown, and while their inhabitants eventually had pensions or were given livings or preferment in the new Church of England, and while their valuables went straight to the royal coffers, books were not valued and great libraries perished as symbols of the old Church. Of those of Glastonbury from which St. Dunstan led the 10th-century monastic revival, or of Malmesbury, home of Celtic scholarship in southern England and of St. Aldhelm, to take but two examples, virtually nothing remains. Even the buildings suffered and became, like Fountains Abbey, quarries of ready-dressed stone for the houses of the new owners.

It was not until Elizabeth's reign that there was any systematic attempt to pick up the pieces. If the motives for the Dissolution were largely political, ironically so too were the motives for the re-collection of what could be salvaged from the dispersal of these libraries. The Elizabethan antiquaries were searching for precedent and for information about the pre-Conquest Church to show that from the time of Augustine onwards the Church *in* England had always really been the Church *of* England and that what the reformers had done was to return to her pristine purity. Matthew Parker, first Anglican Archbishop of Canterbury (1559 to 1575), had as his main concern the regulation of the life of the new church; in his primacy were issued the Thirty-Nine Articles (1562) and instructions on ritual and dress (1566). Less official, but no less important to his work, was his book on the origins of the English Church and the position of the See of Canterbury, *De Antiquitate Britannicæ Ecclesiæ et Privilegiis Ecclesiæ Cantuariensis* (1572). He also published many texts, chiefly in Latin but also including English works such as Ælfric's sermon on the symbolic nature of the Eucharist, which put forward a view which had been condemned in 1070 by the Council of Vercelli in favour of the doctrine of transubstantiation which was abhorred by the reformers. All this was made possible because he was an indefatigable collector of books and manuscripts. (One of his many agents was said to have collected 6700 volumes for him in four years.) The bulk of his collection was not dispersed again on his death but bequeathed to Corpus Christi College, Cambridge, of which he had been Master.

Another indefatigable collector was Sir Robert Cotton (1571–1631). He was at school at Westminster where William Camden was second master, forming an acquaintanceship that was later renewed at meetings of the Antiquarian Society. This society, which was founded in 1572 by Archbishop Parker and others, met regularly at Cotton's house in the 1590s until it was dissolved by James I in 1604 lest its discussions turned to politics; accounts of the papers read at its meetings are preserved in Cotton's collection. Cotton was a collector of manuscripts throughout his life, and his collection grew to such an extent that, despite its uses, it came to be felt a danger to the State in the hands of a private individual. Eventually it was confiscated in 1631, an act which accelerated Cotton's death. Later it was restored to his son and became almost a national collection until it was acquired by the nation in 1700, and an Act of Parliament provided that 'it be kept and preserved by the name of the Cottonian Library for public use and advantage'. It was moved to Essex House in the Strand and in 1730 to Ashburnham House in Little Dean's Yard, Westminster, where it severely suffered in a fire on the 23rd of October 1731. When the British Museum was founded in 1753 it was moved to Bloomsbury where it still remains. In its original arrangement each bookcase was surmounted by a bust of a Roman Emperor, and the designations of the manuscripts still recall the arrangement. Thus the *Beowulf* MS. is known as Cotton Vitellius A XV—number 15 on shelf A of the case with Vitellius on top.

These two collectors illustrate how the preservation and early modern interest in Old English were largely extra-literary. Anglo-Saxon studies remained the province of the amateur until the new interest in the history of English in the 19th century, when the *New* (later called *Oxford*) *English Dictionary* was started and with it the Early English Text Society began publishing its volumes of Old and Middle English texts as source material, and from then on the work of publication and explication has proceeded apace.

THE MANUSCRIPT SOURCES OF OUR TEXTS

1. *Poetry*

All the surviving poetry is presented in two complete scholarly editions: by G. P. Krapp and E. V. K. Dobbie in the six volumes of *Anglo-Saxon Poetic Records*, published in New York by Columbia U.P., 1931–53, and in London by Routledge, 1931–54; and by C. W. M. Grein in *Bibliothek der angelsächsischen Poesie*, 3 volumes, 1893–8. It is unlikely that the beginner will need to consult these. The sources for most of the poems in these volumes are the four main poetical manuscripts: The Beowulf Manuscript, The Exeter Book, The Junius Manuscript, and The Vercelli Book.

THE BEOWULF MANUSCRIPT

Vellum. 209 leaves originally *c.* 23 × 15 cm, but now damaged and much reduced. In the British Museum: MS. Cotton Vitellius A XV.

Contents: The whole consists of two distinct manuscripts bound together in the 16th century. The first is 12th-century, and contains four prose works including Alfred's *Soliloquies*. The second and longer is in a hand of *c.* 1000 and has three prose works followed by *Beowulf* and *Judith*.

History: The first page of the second part has the signature of Laurence Nowell and the date 1563. Nowell (d. 1576) was Dean of Lichfield and a pioneer student of Old English. It passed into Sir Robert Cotton's collection, where it suffered considerable damage in the fire of 1731, and thence to the British Museum with the rest of the collection.

Facsimiles: Early English Text Society, vol. 245, 1959 (*Beowulf* only). Early English Manuscripts in Facsimile, vol. 12, 1964. This series, published in this country by Allen and Unwin, is beyond the pockets of all but the richest libraries and collectors.

Editions: Of all the available editions of *Beowulf* that by C. L. Wrenn (Harrap, 1953, rev. 1958) is the most useful to all but advanced students. *Judith* is edited by B. J. Timmer in Methuen's Old English Library (1952, 2nd ed. 1961).

Translations: Both poems, together with a high proportion of the extant poetry, are in R. G. Gordon, *Anglo-Saxon Poetry* (Everyman, 2nd ed. 1954). Modern translations of *Beowulf* include those by D. Wright (Penguin, 1957), E. T. Donaldson (1967) and K. Crossley-Holland (1968). Although an adaptation, not a translation, *Beowulf* by Rosemary Sutcliff deserves attention (Bodley Head, 1961; publ. Penguin, 1966, as: *Dragon Slayer*).

THE EXETER BOOK

Parchment. 131 leaves, the first eight being 16th-century or later, 31 × 22 cm. Written in the West Country early in the period 970–90, and given to the library of Exeter Cathedral, where it still remains, by Bishop Leofric (d. 1072).

Contents: Almost three dozen separate items including: *Christ, Juliana, The Wanderer, The Seafarer, Widsith, The Fates of Men, Deor, Wulf and Eadwacer, The Wife's Lament, The Descent into Hell, The Husband's Message* and *The Ruin* besides other less noteworthy poems and several groups of riddles and gnomic sayings.

Facsimile: The Exeter Book of Old English Poetry, with introductory chapters (1933).

Editions: Complete, with translations, in the Early English Text Society, Vol. 1 by I. Gollancz (E.E.T.S. 104, 1895); Vol. 2 by W. S. Mackie (E.E.T.S. 194, 1934). Selected modern editions of individual poems include:

Juliana, by Rosemary Woolf (Methuen's Old English Library 1955).

The Wanderer, by R. F. Leslie (Manchester U.P., 1955);

by T. P. Dunning & A. J. Bliss (Methuen's O.E. Library, 1969).

The Seafarer, by I. L. Gordon (Methuen's O.E. Library, 1960).

Widsith, by K. Malone (Methuen's O.E. Library, 1936; 2nd ed. Copenhagen, 1962);

by R. W. Chambers (C.U.P., 1912) [Not modern, but a monumental edition.]

Deor, by K. Malone (Methuen's O.E. Library, 3rd ed. 1961).

The Wife's Lament, The Husband's Message & Ruin in *Three Old English Elegies* edited by R. F. Leslie (Manchester U.P., 1961).

Translations: Most of these items are in Gordon's *Anglo-Saxon Poetry,* and several in Michael Alexander's *The Earliest English Poems* (Penguin, 1966).

THE JUNIUS MANUSCRIPT

Parchment. 116 leaves, 31 × 19 cm. Written by four scribes *c.*1000. In the Bodleian Library, Oxford: MS. Junius 11.

History: The Irish Archbishop Ussher gave it to Francis Junius (1589–1677), a Huguenot pioneer of Old English and related languages, and librarian to the Earl of Arundel. He published the contents in Amsterdam in 1655, attributing them to Cædmon. It was part of his bequest to the University of Oxford.

Contents: Genesis, Exodus, Daniel, Christ and Satan.

Facsimile: The Cædmon Manuscript of Anglo-Saxon Biblical Poetry, Junius XI, in the Bodleian Library (1927).

Editions: The Later Genesis, ed. B. J. Timmer (2nd ed., 1954). *Exodus,* ed. E. B. Irving (Yale U.P., 1953).

Parchment. 137 leaves, 31 × 20 cm. Written in England in an Anglo-Irish hand of the latter part of the 10th century, but now preserved in the Cathedral Chapter Library at Vercelli in Northern Italy: Cod. CXVII. Vercelli is on the pilgrim route to Rome and the manuscript was in the area in the 11th century, for additions made to it then have now been shown to be Italian.

Contents: Twenty-two homilies and a life of St. Guthlac in prose, and six poems: *Andreas, The Fates of the Apostles, Soul and Body I, Homiletic Fragment I, The Dream of the Rood* and *Elene.*

Facsimile: Il Codice Vercellese con Omelie e Poesie in Lingua Anglo-Sassone (Rome, 1913).

Editions:
Andreas & *Fates of the Apostles,* by K. R. Brooks (Oxford, 1961).
Dream of the Rood, by B. Dickins and A. S. C. Ross (Methuen's O.E. Library, 4th ed., 1954).
Elene, by P. O. E. Gradon (Methuen's O.E. Library, 1958).

OTHER POEMS

Bede's Death Song is found only in manuscripts of Cuthbert's letter to Cuthwin describing Bede's last days and death, which is attached to some manuscripts of Bede's *Historia Ecclesiastica.* Cædmon's *Hymn* is added in some manuscripts to the passage which we quoted at the beginning of Chapter 6 where Bede tells of Cædmon's gift, and paraphrases his song. Both poems are edited by A. H. Smith in *Three Northumbrian Poems* (Methuen's Old English Library, 1933, rev. 1968).

Battle of Maldon. The 11th-century manuscript, originally in the Cottonian Collection, was virtually destroyed in the fire of 1731. A transcript had, however, been made previously by John Elphinston, the under-keeper, which attempted to reproduce the form as well as the substance of the poem. It was printed by Thomas Hearne in 1726, and itself passed eventually to the Bodleian where it was identified before the last war. Before it was destroyed, the original manuscript had also passed through many hands: John Leland is the first recorded owner after the Dissolution, later Archbishop Parker had it and printed Asser's *Life of King Alfred* which was in the same volume, but it did not go with the rest of his collection when he died; in 1600 it was in the library of Lord Lumley, and only then did it go to Cotton. The transcript is edited by E. V. Gordon (Methuen's Old English Library, 1937) and the poem with a translation facing is printed in M. Ashdown, *English and Norse Documents relating to the Reign of Ethelred the Unready* (C.U.P., 1930).

Battle of Brunanburh. This poem of 74 lines is found in five of the seven manuscripts of the *Anglo-Saxon Chronicle* under the year 937. It is edited by A. Campbell (1938).

Waldere. The vellum fragments are in the Royal Library at Copenhagen, where they were discovered in 1860. It is edited by F. Norman (Methuen's Old English Library, 1933).

2. *Prose*

Manuscripts of prose works are generally more common; our treatment of each is therefore briefer. There is a complete edition of the prose in progress corresponding to Grein's edition of the poetry: *Bibliothek der angelsächischen Prosa*, 1872–, originally edited by C. W. M. Grein and R. Wülker and now by H. Hecht. But for most of our readers the passages in readers will probably suffice.

KING ALFRED

The *Cura Pastoralis* survived in seven manuscripts until modern times. The copy sent to Bishop Wærferth at Worcester is now at Oxford in the Bodleian (MS. Hatton 20). It is reproduced in Early English Manuscripts in Facsimile, Vol. 6 (1956). The bequest of Francis Junius brought another manuscript to the Bodleian (MS. Junius 53). It is a copy of MS. Cotton Tiberius B XI which was reduced to fragments by the fire of 1731, though another manuscript survived (Otho B II). There are also three manuscripts in Cambridge: at Corpus Christi College in Archbishop Parker's collection, at Trinity College, and in the University Library. It was edited by H. Sweet (E.E.T.S. 45 & 50, 1871–2, repr.

1958). The Preface on the state of learning is in many readers.

There are two Old English manuscripts of *Orosius*: the Lauderdale (at Helmingham Hall in Suffolk) which is contemporary but incomplete, and a 10th- or 11th-century one which found its way into Cotton's collection (MS. Cotton Tiberius B I). This manuscript was twice transcribed by early scholars. The Lauderdale MS. is reproduced in Vol. 3 of Early English Manuscripts in Facsimile (1953), and the text was edited with the Latin original by H. Sweet (E.E.T.S. 79, 1883).

Bede's *History* has five manuscripts. The oldest and best is MS. Tanner 10 in the Bodleian; Corpus Christi College, Cambridge, has two from Archbishop Parker (MSS. 41 and 279); The British Museum has the fragmentary MS. Cotton Otho B XI, and there is one in Cambridge University Library (MS. Kk. 3. 18). The standard edition is that by T. Miller in four volumes with a translation (E.E.T.S. 95–6, 110–11; 1890–8). It is also Vol. 4 of the *Bibliothek* (1899).

Boethius' *De Consolatione Philosophiae* is another work that suffered in the Cottonian fire, when the early 10th-century MS. Cotton Otho A VI was damaged. The most complete manuscript is thus the early 12th-century MS. Bodl. 180 in the Bodleian. Unlike Cotton Otho which has the verse passages (*Metra*) as verse, this has them in prose. Junius transcribed the Cotton manuscript well before the fire. The text is edited (Oxford, 1899) and translated (Oxford, 1900) by W. J. Sedgefield.

We have already noted that St. Augustine's *Soliloquies* is in the first portion of the *Beowulf* manuscript (MS. Cotton Vitellius A XV). There is also a transcript of it by Junius in the Bodleian. It is Vol. 11 (1922) of the *Bibliothek*. Other editions are much less satisfactory. It was translated by H. L. Hargrove (New York, 1904).

THE ANGLO-SAXON CHRONICLE

Seven manuscripts came down to modern times, but only six now survive. They are designated by letters of the alphabet for convenience of reference.

A   The 'Parker Chronicle' is at Corpus Christi College, Cambridge, like most of Parker's other manuscripts (MS. 173). It is in one hand as far as the entry for 891, then in a variety of hands until the entry for 1001. It was continued at Canterbury from 1005 to 1070. It is reproduced in E.E.T.S. 208 (1941). An 11th-century copy of A was destroyed in the Cottonian fire; it had been transcribed in part (now at Trinity College, Dublin) and also published.

B B.M. MS. Cotton Tiberius A VI. Written *c*. 1000, its last entry is for 977.

C B.M. MS. Cotton Tiberius B I. This is a copy of B which was made at Abingdon *c*. 1055, and continued to the entry for 1066.

D The 'Worcester Chronicle', B.M. MS. Cotton Tiberius B IV of *c*. 1100. It stops at 1079. It includes the Mercian chronicle and also a Northumbrian version for 733–806, and some pieces of Bede.

E The 'Peterborough Chronicle'. Now in the Bodleian (MS. Laud Misc. 636). It is a copy of an original from Canterbury made after a fire at Peterborough in 1121, and was continued there until 1154. It is therefore the last of the surviving manuscripts to be maintained. R. W. Chambers placed the dividing line between Old and Middle English between its entries for 1131 and for 1132. It is reproduced in Vol. 4 of *Early English Manuscripts in Facsimile* (1954). Both D and E are related to a Northern text of the Chronicle, probably from York.

F B.M. Cotton Domitian A VIII has very little independent value. It is a copy of the archetype of E made at Canterbury *c*. 1100. Though it adds local traditions, it abbreviates and translates parts into Latin.

The list of modern editions and translations is almost as complicated. The standard edition is *Two of the Saxon Chronicles Parallel* edited by C. Plummer in two volumes (Oxford, 1892–9). This edition is translated page for page by G. N. Garmonsway in Everyman's Library (2nd ed., 1960). See also *The Anglo-Saxon Chronicle* translated by D. Whitelock, D. C. Douglas and S. I. Tucker (1961).

ÆLFRIC

So far Ælfric has suffered neglect by modern editors, though this is being remedied by P. Clemoes for the Early English Text Society. The two series of *Catholic Homilies* were edited and translated by B. Thorpe in the two volumes of *The Homilies of the Anglo-Saxon Church* (1844–6), and the 'Sermon on the Sacrifice on Easter Day' had been printed by Archbishop Parker. The *Lives of Saints* were edited in four volumes with facing translations by W. W. Skeat (E.E.T.S. 76, 82, 94, 114; 1881–1900). There is a facsimile of one manuscript of the First Series (B.M. Royal 7C) in Vol. 13 of Early English Manuscripts in Facsimile (1966). The one work of Ælfric that is most readily available is the anonymous gloss to his *Colloquium* from B.M. MS. Cotton Tiberius A III. It is edited by G. N. Garmonsway in Methuen's Old English Library (2nd ed., 1947).

WULFSTAN

Twenty-five homilies have been attributed to Wulfstan in whole or part. They are edited by D. Bethurum in *The Homilies of Wulfstan* (Oxford, 1957). *Sermo Lupi ad Anglos*, his most famous homily, exists in five manuscripts. It is edited by D. Whitelock in Methuen's Old English Library (3rd ed., 1963), and translated in *English Historical Documents*, Vol. 1 (1955).

SCIENTIFIC WRITINGS

Though we have not discussed Old English scientific texts, some may like to look at this *genre* of educational works. The best and most easily available is Byrhtferth's *Manual* which is edited and translated by S. J. Crawford from the unique 10th-century manuscript in the Bodleian Library (MS. Ashmole 328). Many medical texts are edited and translated in O. Cockayne, *Leech-doms, Wortcunning and Starcraft of Early England* in the Rolls Series (3 vols. 1864–6) which may not be all that easy to come across.

Excerpts with Translation

Neque enim possunt carmina, quamvis optime composita, ex alia in aliam linguam ad verbum sine detrimento sui decoris ac dignitatis transferri.   Bede HIST. ECCL. IV. xxiv

It is impossible to translate poetry, no matter how excellent, word for word from one language to another without losing its beauty and style.

Despite Bede's *caveat*, most of the pieces in this second part are in translation. They are neither elegant nor poetic, but our translations do provide a short cut to the literature we have been discussing. The following three short passages, however, which we print in the original, may serve as some indication of how short a cut it is, and give some idea of what Old English looks like. There are two striking differences from modern English. The first, and more superficial, is the use of three special characters. They are:

    Æ, æ, æsc 'ash'=a   as *cat* (short) and *air* (long)
    Ð, ð, eð 'eth'=th
      Þ, þ, thorn=th
Some texts also use two more:
      Ƿ, ƿ, wynn=w
      Ȝ, ȝ, yogh=g
and the abbreviation ⁊=and.

The second difference is more fundamental. Old English is an inflected language. This means that the shape of words can vary with their function in the sentence. Syntax and word order are also affected in that relationships between words can be shown directly.

a. Narrative prose. *The Anglo-Saxon Chronicle*

Anno dcclxxi. Hēr cuōm se here tō Rēadingum on West-Seaxe, ond þæs ymb iii niht ridon ii eorlas ūp. Þā gemētte hīe Æþelwulf aldormon on Englafelda, ond him þær wiþ gefeaht, ond sige nam. Þæs ymb iii niht Æþered cyning ond Ælfred his brōþur þær micle fierd to Readingum gelæddon, ond wiþ þone here gefuhton, ond þær wæs micel wæl geslægen on gehwæþre hond, ond Æþelwulf aldormon wearþ ofslægen; ond þā Deniscan āhton wælstōwe gewald.

Translation:

871   In this year the Danish army came to Reading in Wessex, and after three days two Viking leaders rode up. Then Athelwulf, the alderman, went out against them at Engelfield, and fought with them and took the victory. After three days King Athered and his brother Alfred led a great force to Reading and fought with the Danish army, and there was much slaughter made on both sides, and Athelwulf, the alderman, was slain, and the Danes retained control of the battlefield.

b. Alliterative prose. The opening of Ælfric's *Life of King Oswald*

Æfter ðan ðe Augustīnus tō Engla lande becōm, wæs sum æðele cyning, Ōswold gehāten, on Norðhymbra lande, gelȳfed swȳþe on God. Sē fērde on his iugoðe fram his frēondum and māgum to Scotlande on sǣ, and þær sōna wearð gefullod, and his gefēran samod þe mid him sīþedon. Betwux þām wearð ofslagen Ēadwine his ēam, Norðhymbra cynincg, on Crīst gelȳfed, fram Brytta cyninge, Ceadwalla gecīged, and twegen his æftergengan binnan twām gēarum; and se Ceadwalla slōh and tō sceame tūcode þā Norðhymbran lēode œfter heora hlāfordes fylle, oð þæt Ōswold se ēadiga his yfelnysse ādwǣscte.

Translation:

After Augustine had come to England, there was a certain noble king, called Oswold, in the land of the Northumbrians, a firm believer in God. He journeyed in his youth away from his friends and family to Scotland [*i.e.* Ireland] by sea, and there was soon baptised, and [so were] his companions also who had made the journey with him. Meanwhile his uncle Edwin, the king of the Northumbrians, a believer in Christ, was killed by the British king, called Ceadwalla, and [so were] two of his successors within two years; and this Ceadwalla slew and shamefully ill-treated the Northumbrian people after the fall of their lord, until the blessed Oswold quenched his evil-doing.

c. *Beowulf*, ll. 32–52. The Funeral of Scyld Shefing

    Þǣr æt hȳðe stōd   hringedstefna
    īsig ond ūtfūs,   æþelinges fær;
    ālēdon þā   lēofne þēoden,
35 bēaga bryttan   on bearm scipes,
    mǣrne be mæste.   Þǣr wæs mādma fela
    of feorwegum   frætwa gelǣded;
    ne hȳrde ic cȳmlicor   cēol gegyrwan
    hildewǣpnum   ond heaðowǣdum,
40 billum ond byrnum;   him on bearme læg
    mādma mænigo,   þā him mid scoldon
    on flōdes ǣht   feor gewītan.
    Nalæs hī hine lǣssan   lācum tēodan,
    þēodgestrēonum,   þon þā dydon,
45 þē hine æt frumsceafte   forð onsendon
    ǣnne ofer ȳðe   umborwesende.
    Þā gȳt hīe him āsetton   segen gyldenne
    hēah ofer hēafod,   lēton holm beran,
    gēafon on gārsecg;   him wæs geōmor sefa,
50 murnende mōd.   Men ne cunnon
    secgan tō sōðe,   selerǣdende,
    hæleð under heofenum,   hwā þǣm hlæste onfēng.

Beowulf, ll. 32–52. *Translation:*

The ring-prowed ship stood there in the harbour,
ice-covered and eager to set out, the prince's vessel;
then they laid their beloved lord,
the giver of rings, down in the bosom of the boat,   [35
the illustrious man against the mast. There was a
   quantity of treasure,

of precious things brought from distant parts.
I have never heard of a ship more comelier equipped
with battle-weapons and war-dress,
with swords and corslets. On his breast lay   [40
a multitude of treasures which with him were about to
go far in the sea's possession.
By no means did they provide him with fewer gifts,
treasures of the people, than did those
who in the beginning sent him forth   [45
alone over the waves when he was yet a child.
Furthermore they set him a golden standard
high over his head, allowed the sea to bear him,
gave him to the ocean; their hearts were sad,
their minds mournful. Men cannot   [50
truly say, counsellors in hall,
heroes under the heavens, who received that cargo.

Translations from the Old English

King Alfred commands that Bishop Wærferth be greeted with his words in love and friendship. I want you to know that I have often considered what learned men there used to be through the English nation both in religious and secular life; and how there were blessed times then throughout England; and how the kings who ruled the people in those days obeyed God and his priests; and how they preserved their peace, their morality and their authority within their kingdom, and also enlarged their territory abroad; and how they had success in both war and learning; and also how eager the members of holy orders were to teach and learn and perform all the duties which they owed to God; and how foreigners came here to this country to find wisdom and learning; and how we must now obtain it from abroad if we wish to possess it.

So general was this decay in England that there were very few on this side of the Humber who could understand the meaning of their mass-books or translate a letter from Latin into English; and I believe that there were not many beyond the Humber. There were so few that I cannot think of even a single one south of the Thames when I came to the throne. Thanks be to God Almighty that we now have any supply of teachers at all. And therefore I command you, as I believe you will, to disengage yourself from worldly affairs as often as you can, so that you put to use, whenever you are able, the wisdom that God has given you. Consider what punishments are due to us if in this present life we have neither loved knowledge ourselves nor allowed it to other men. We merely love the name, and very few of us the obligations, of being Christians.

When I considered all this, I also remembered how, before it was all plundered and destroyed by fire, I saw the churches throughout all England were filled with treasures and books and a great multitude of God's servants; and they had very little knowledge of those books because they could understand nothing of them, for they were not written in their own language. It was as if they said: 'Our ancestors, who once possessed these places, loved wisdom, and because of this they acquired wealth and left it to us. Here one can still see their footsteps, but we do not know how to follow them; therefore we have now lost both the wealth and the wisdom because we would not turn our minds to that track.'

When I thought of all this, I wondered very greatly about the just and wise men who used to live throughout England, and who studied all those books perfectly, why they did not translate any part of them into their own language. But I soon found an answer and said: 'They did not think that men would ever become so careless, and learning fall into such decay; they refrained from translation deliberately, and intended that there should be more wisdom in the land the more languages we knew.'

Then I remembered that the law was first found in Hebrew, and afterwards the Greeks learnt it and translated it into their own language, and all the other books as well. And afterwards the Romans did the same: when they had learnt it they translated it all into their own language with the help of learned interpreters. And also all the other Christian nations translated a part of them into their own languages. Therefore it seems better to me, if you agree, that we too translate certain books, which are most essential for all men to know, into the language we all know, and bring it about, as we may easily do with God's help if we have peace, that all the sons of free men in England now who have the means to apply themselves to it be set to the task of learning, for as long as they cannot be of use in any other employment, until the time that they can understand written English well. After that one may teach further in Latin those whom one wishes to have more instruction and to promote to a higher level.

When I considered how the teaching of Latin had previously decayed in England, and yet many could read writing in English, I began amidst the various and manifold troubles of this kingdom to translate into English the book which is called in Latin *Pastoralis*, and in English *Shepherd's Book*, sometimes word for word and sometimes by paraphrase, as I was taught by my archbishop Plegmund, my bishop Asser, and my priests Grimbold and John. After I had learned it, as I understood it and might recount it most intelligibly, I translated it into English. And I will send a copy to every bishopric in my kingdom; and in each book there will be a book-marker worth fifty mancuses. And I command in God's name that no one should take the marker from the book, or the book from the monastery—it is unknown for how long there will be such learned bishops as now, thanks be to God, there are everywhere. Therefore I desire that the book should always remain at that place unless the bishop wishes to have it with him, or it is on loan somewhere, or someone is copying it.

'THE ANGLO-SAXON CHRONICLE'

[The story of Cynewulf and Cyneheard from the entry for 755 is the highlight of the earlier part of the *Chronicle*, though its prose is less disciplined than that of later parts. The translation does not attempt to disguise this.]

755 In this year because of Sigebryht's unlawful actions Cynewulf and the councillors of Wessex deprived him of all his lands except for Hampshire; he kept this until he slew the chief who had stayed faithful to him longest. Then Cynewulf expelled him to the Weald, and he lived there until a herdsman stabbed him to death by the stream at Privett, and thus avenged the chief, Cumbra.

And that same Cynewulf often fought great battles against the Welsh, and after about thirty-one years of his reign he wished to expel a noble called Cyneheard—and this Cyneheard was the brother of that same Sigebryht. And then Cyneheard heard that the king was staying with a mistress near Merton accompanied by a small troop, and he surrounded him there and besieged the house before the men who were with the king discovered he was there.

And then the king became aware of this and went to the door, and nobly defended himself until he saw the nobleman and rushed out at him, severely wounding him. And then they all fought the king until they had killed him. And then the king's thanes discovered the disturbance from the woman's screams, and then those who were ready and quickest ran there. And the noble offered each of them property and their life, and each of them refused; but they continued the fight until they all lay dead, except one Welsh hostage, and he was sorely wounded.

In the morning when the king's thanes who had been left behind heard that the king was slain they rode there—his chief Osric, his thane Wiferth, and the men whom he had left behind—and discovered Cyneheard in the dwelling where the king lay slain (and they had locked themselves in), and they approached the place. And then he offered them their choice of money or land if they would grant him the kingship and said that there were kinsmen of theirs amongst them who were unwilling to leave. And they replied that there was no kinsman dearer to them than their lord, and they would never follow his murderer. And then they offered to let their kinsmen depart in safety; and they replied that the same had been offered to the companions who were with the king before. Then they said that they did not care for this 'any more than did your companions who were slain with the king'. And then they went on fighting around the gate until they entered the walls and killed the noble; and then they slew all the warriors with him, except one who was his godson; and he was granted his life although he had suffered many wounds.

[More typical are entries like these recording the Danish wars.]

865 In this year a heathen force remained in Thanet and made peace with the people of Kent, and the Kentishmen promised them money in return for peace; and under cover of peace and the contract of money the troop went stealthily by night and completely ravaged the eastern district of Kent.

866 In this year Æthelred, the brother of Æthelbryht, came to the throne in Wessex. And in the same year a great army

arrived in the country of the English nation, and made winter quarters in East Anglia, and there were provided with horses; and they made peace with the people.

867 In this year the army journeyed from East Anglia across the mouth of the Humber to the city of York in Northumbria. And there was great discord amongst the people themselves, and they deposed their king Osbryht, and took Ælla, who was not of royal stock, in his place. And it was late in the year that they turned to making war on the army; and yet they assembled a large force, and then sought the enemy at York; and they forced their way into the city and some of them reached the inside. And there was immense slaughter of Northumbrians, some inside the city and some outside the walls, and both kings were slain; and the survivors made peace with the raiding force.

ÆLFRIC'S 'LIFE OF ST. EDMUND'

A very learned monk came south over the sea from Saint Benedict's monastery in King Æthelred's day to Archbishop Dunstan three years before he died. And the monk was called Abbo. Then they talked together until Dunstan told the tale of Saint Edmund, as Edmund's swordbearer had recounted it to King Æthelstan when Dunstan was a very young man and the swordbearer was very old. Then the monk wrote all the narrative into a book, and afterwards when the book came to us within a few years we translated it into English as it remains ever since. Then after two years monk Abbo returned to his monastery and was soon made abbot of that same place.

Holy Edmund, king of the East Anglians, was wise and worthy and always honoured Almighty God with noble virtues. He was humble and virtuous and remained so resolute that he would not turn to shameful vices, nor bend his moral standards in any direction, but had always in mind the true doctrine: 'If you are appointed ruler, do not exalt yourself, but amongst men behave as one of them.' He was as kind as a father to paupers and widows, and always guided his people with benevolence to righteousness, and restrained the cruel, and lived blessedly in the true faith.

Then it happened at last that the Danes journeyed with their fleet, plundering and killing far and wide throughout the land as their custom is. In that fleet the first in command were Hinguar and Hubba, united by the Devil, and they landed with their warships in Northumberland, and laid waste the land and slaughtered the people. Then Hinguar turned east with his ships, and Hubba remained in Northumberland, having won victory with cruelty. Then Hinguar rowed on and arrived in East Anglia in the year in which prince Alfred, who afterwards became the famous king of the West Saxons, was twenty-one years old. Then the above-mentioned Hinguar, just like a wolf, suddenly stole on land and slew the people, men, women and innocent children, and with shameful ignominy murdered blameless Christians. Then immediately afterwards he sent a boastful message to the king, saying that he should submit to his allegiance if he valued his life. Then the messenger came to King Edmund and boldly announced Hinguar's message to him: 'Our king, Hinguar, brave and victorious on sea and land, rules many peoples, and now comes with an army here into this land to take up winter quarters with his soldiers. He now commands you quickly to share your hidden stores of gold and your ancestral treasures with him, and become his tributary king, if you wish to stay alive, for you have no power to withstand him.'

Well, then King Edmund called to him the bishop who was nearest at hand, and considered with him how he should reply to the cruel Hinguar. Then the bishop, fearing for the sudden emergency and for the king's life, said that he thought it advisable to submit to Hinguar's demands. Then the king fell silent, and stared at the ground, and at last spoke to him like a king: 'Oh thou bishop, these wretched countrymen are shamefully afflicted, and I would prefer to fall in battle, provided my people may enjoy their native land.' And the bishop replied: 'Beloved King, your people lie slain, and you do not have the troops with whom you can fight. And the warriors from the sea will come and bind you alive unless you save your life by flight or submission.' Then King Edmund, as he was a brave man, said: 'It is my desire and wish not to remain alone alive after my beloved thanes who were taken by surprise and murdered in their beds with their children and their wives by these pirates. It has never been my custom to flee, and I would rather die, if needs be, for my own native land; Almighty God knows that I will never turn from worshipping Him, nor from His true love, whether I die or live.'

After these words he turned to the messenger whom Hinguar had sent to him, and bravely said to him: 'Now truly you are worthy to be slain, but I do not wish to defile my clean hands with your foul blood, because I follow Christ who taught us by his example, and I will happily be killed by you if God so ordains it. Go now without delay, and tell your cruel lord: "While he lives Edmund will never yield to Hinguar, the heathen general, unless he first submits in faith to Christ the Saviour in this land".' Then the messenger quickly went away, and met the cruel Hinguar on the road hastening to Edmund, and he told the wicked man how he was answered. Then Hinguar arrogantly commanded the pirates to look out for the king alone, who scorned his command, and bind him immediately.

Well, when Hinguar arrived, King Edmund stood within his hall, thinking of the Saviour, and threw aside his weapon; he wanted to imitate the example of Christ who forbade Peter to fight the cruel Jews with weapons. Well, then the wicked warriors bound Edmund, and insulted him shamefully, and beat him with rods, and immediately afterwards led out the devout king to a solitary deeply rooted tree, and tied him to it with harsh thongs, and then again scourged him for a long time with whips; and between the blows he constantly called out with true faith to Christ his Saviour. And then the pagans became mad with anger at his faith because he called to Christ for help. Then they shot at him with javelins, as if for sport, until he was completely covered with their spears like the spines of a hedghog, just as Sebastian was. Then Hinguar, the wicked sailor, saw that the noble king would not renounce Christ, but with resolute faith always called out to Him. Then he ordered his head to be struck off, and the pagans obeyed. While he was still calling to Christ, the heathens dragged the holy man to slaughter, and with a single stroke struck off his head, and his soul journeyed rejoicing to Christ. There was a certain man nearby, kept hidden from the heathens by God, who heard all this and afterwards related it as we tell it here.

Well, then the pirates returned to the ships, and hid the head of the holy Edmund in thick brambles, so that it would not be buried. Then after a time after they had gone away, the countrymen—those who survived—came to the place where their lord's body lay headless, and grieved for his death in their hearts, and especially because they did not have the head for the body. Then the witness who had seen it said that the pirates took the head with them, and that it seemed to him, as in fact was entirely true, that they had hidden the head somewhere in the wood.

Then they all went together to the wood, searching everywhere through bushes and brambles to see if they might find that head anywhere. Also there was a great miracle that a wolf was sent by God's direction to protect that head from other wild animals by day and night. Then they went about searching and continually calling as is the habit of those who often walk in a wood: 'Where are you now, Companion?' And the head answered them: 'Here, here, here.' And as often as any of them shouted so it called in answer until, because of the calling, they arrived at the spot where he was. Then the grey wolf that guarded the head lay with its two paws clasped about it, greedy and hungry, but not daring to eat it for fear of God, and protecting it instead against wild animals. Then they were astonished at the wolf's guardianship, and took that blessed head home with them, giving thanks to God for all his wonders. But the wolf followed on after the head, as if he were tame, until they came to the town, and then he returned to the wood.

Then the country people laid the head with the saintly body, and buried him as best they could in haste, and immediately afterwards built a church above his grave. Then after the space of many years when the ravaging had ceased and peace was granted to the afflicted people they joined together and built a splendid church for the saint, because miracles frequently took place at his tomb and the chapel where he was buried. Then they wanted to exhume the holy body with public honour and lay him inside the church. It was a great miracle that he was just as whole as if he were alive, with an incorrupt body, and his neck, which had been severed, was healed and it was as if there were a silken thread around his neck to show men how he was slain. And also the wounds which the cruel heathens inflicted on his body with numerous spears were healed by the power of God in heaven; and he lies thus uncorrupted until the present day, awaiting the Resurrection and eternal wonders. His body, which lies undecayed, shows us that he lived chastely in this world, and journeyed to Christ with a blameless life.

[The remainder of the *Life* records the miracles associated with the saint's tomb.]

WULFSTAN'S 'ADDRESS TO THE ENGLISH'

[Ælfric's prose is hard enough to reproduce in modern English; Wulfstan's *hwyl* is almost impossible. Nor is the content of the *Sermo Lupi ad Anglos*, 'gang bang' and all, compelling enough to readers brought up on the *News of the World*. We therefore include only the opening paragraphs as an example of his writing.]

Beloved men, understand that this is the truth: the world is in haste, and approaches the end; this is why things in this world grow worse with time, and on account of the sins of the people they must needs thus grow more evil daily until the arrival of Antichrist; and it will indeed be a cruel and terrible time then throughout the earth.

Be sure of this too: that the devil has for many a year led this people far too far astray, and there was little faith to be found among men, though their speech was fair. Wrong-doing was far too rampant in the land, and few there who sought a solution as eagerly as they ought. But day by day men piled evil upon evil; wrong-doing reared up, and many an injustice too, all too widely throughout the whole nation. And we also therefore have experienced many an injury and ignominy; and if we are to experience a remedy then we must earn it from God better than we have done up to now. Our great efforts have earned us the misery that now attends us; it will take exceedingly great efforts if we are to receive a remedy at God's hands, and things are to get better in the future. Certainly we know full well that a great sin requires great satisfaction, and a great fire no little water if a man is to quite quench it. And great is the need for every man to eagerly observe God's law henceforward better than he did before, and duly perform his duty to God.

'BEOWULF'

Beowulf and Grendel's Mother

Then they fell to sleep. One paid dearly for his night's rest, as had so often happened since the time Grendel inhabited the gold-hall, performed wrong deeds, until the end came, death after his crimes. It became apparent, widely known among the people, that an avenger lived on after the wicked foe, for a long time after the terrible strife: Grendel's mother, a monster among women, brooded over her misery. She was decreed to dwell in the fearful water, the chill streams, after Cain murdered his only brother, his father's son, with the sword. Cain then went about as an outlaw, branded for murder; fleeing from the joys of men, he dwelt in the wilderness. To him were born many fated spirits; one of these was Grendel, a hateful and savage outcast, who had found at Heorot a man wide awake waiting for the fight. The monster laid hold of him, yet the warrior kept in mind the power of his strength, the generous gift which God granted him, and he trusted in the Almighty for mercy, help and support. Because of this he overcame the fiend, struck down the spirit from hell. Then the enemy of mankind went away abjectly, deprived of joy to seek his death place. And in spite of this, his mother, ravenous and gloomy, planned to make the sorrowful journey to avenge the death of her son.

So she arrived at Heorot, where the Ring-Danes slept all over the hall. There was a change of fortune for the nobles as soon as Grendel's mother came within. The terror she created was less only as much as a woman's skill and prowess in war is compared with a man's, when the ornamented sword, hammer-forged, the blood-stained blade with trusty edge, cleaves the boar image on the enemy's helmet. Then in the hall the hard-edged sword was taken down from above the benches. Many a broad sword was raised, firmly gripped in the hand. When terror seized them they forgot about the helmet and mighty mail-coat. She was in a hurry, wanted to be away from there, to save her life when she had been discovered. Quickly she firmly seized one of the nobles, and went away to the marshes. It was Hrothgar's warrior most famed between the two seas, a mighty shield-warrior, a glorious hero, whom she destroyed in his resting place. Beowulf was not there; before then after the distribution of treasures other quarters were allotted to the noble Geat. There was uproar in Heorot. She removed Grendel's arm, that she knew so well, covered in blood. Sorrow was renewed, returned once more to the dwellings. It was no good exchange for both sides to pay with the lives of loved ones.

The wise old king, the grey-haired warrior, was sad at heart, when he learnt that the counsellor most dear to him was dead—deprived of life. Beowulf, the victorious hero, was quickly summoned to the chamber. At daybreak the noble champion went with his retainers, accompanied by his comrades, to the place where the wise king waited, to see if the Almighty would ever bring about a change for him after the tale of woe. Then the man, distinguished in battle, went across the floor with his small troop—the hall timbers resounded—in order to greet the wise lord of the descendants of Ing, to ask if the night had been as agreeable as he desired.

Hrothgar, the protector of the Scyldings, spoke: 'Do not talk about happiness; sorrow has returned to the Danish people. Æschere is dead, Yrmenlaf's elder brother, my trusted counsellor, my adviser and comrade when we defended our lives in battle, when the troops fought and hewed at the boar-crests. He was such a man as a noble should be; he was a most excellent chief. The wandering and murderous spirit slaughtered him in Heorot. I do not know to what place the terrible creature returned, rejoicing in her carrion, gladdened by the feast. She has avenged the feud begun when last night you killed Grendel violently with your harsh grip because he had over a long time reduced and destroyed my people. He fell in the fight, having forfeited his life; now another powerful evil-doer has come, wishing to avenge her kinsman. She has carried the feud far, as may be seen from many a thane who grieves for his treasure-giver in his heart, a harsh sorrow. Now the hand which helped your almost every wish lies still.

'I have heard the country dwellers, my people, the counsellors in hall, say that they saw two such mighty wanderers of the waste-land, alien spirits, guarding the moors. One of these, as far as they could tell most clearly, resembled a woman. The other wretched one trod the paths of exile in the form of a man, except that he was larger than any other mortal. In days gone by my people named him Grendel. They knew of no father, whether they had any, begotten on mysterious spirits. They dwell in a hidden land with wolf-infested hillsides, windswept headlands, treacherous paths through the fen, where the mountain stream flows down-wards under the mists of the cliffs, a flood beneath the earth. It is not many miles from here that the lake stands, over which hang frost-covered groves; a deeply rooted forest overshadows the water. There every night a fearful wonder can be seen—fire on the water. There is no son of man alive who is so wise that he knows its depths. Although the heath-stalker, the sturdy-horned hart, harassed by hounds, makes for the forest, chased from afar, he would rather forfeit his life on its bank than plunge in to save himself. It is no safe place. From the lake turbulent waves rise up darkly towards the clouds when the wind stirs up a fearful storm, until the sky grows gloomy and the heavens weep.

'Now once again we are dependent on you alone for help. You do not know the region, the fearful place, where you may find the sinful creature. Seek it if you dare; I will reward you with riches, ancient treasure, braided gold, for the conflict if you escape, as I did before.'

Beowulf, the son of Ecgtheow, spoke: 'Do not grieve, wise man! It is better for everyone to avenge his comrade than to mourn much. Each of us must expect an end to life in this world. He, who can, should endeavour to win glory before his death; that is best afterwards for a dead warrior. Rise up, guardian of the kingdom. Let us go quickly, and look for the track of Grendel's kinswoman. I promise you she will not escape to cover, neither in the depth of the earth, nor in the mountain wood, nor to the bottom of the ocean, go where she will! Today have patience in all your misfortunes, as I am sure you will.'

Then the old man leapt up, thanked God, the Mighty Lord, for what the man had said. Then a horse, a steed with plaited mane, was bridled for Hrothgar. The wise prince went forward in stately fashion; the infantry of shield-bearers advanced. Along the forest paths footsteps were clearly visible, tracks along the ground. She held straight on across the dark moor, carrying the lifeless thane, the best of those who watched over the stronghold with Hrothgar. Then the sons of nobles traversed the steep and rocky slopes, the narrow paths, the rocky tracks—an unknown way—precipitous cliffs, many dwellings of water monsters. With a few skilled men he went on ahead to view the region, until suddenly he discovered mountain trees overhanging a grey rock, a joyless forest. The water was beneath, blood-stained and turbulent. It was a grievous thing for all the Danes, the friends of the Scyldings, many a thane, to suffer in their hearts—sorrow for each of the nobles—after they discovered Æschere's head on the cliff by the lake. The water surged with blood, with hot gore; the people gazed on it. Time and again the horn sang out an eager war song. The warriors all sat down. Then they saw in the water many of the serpent breed, wondrous sea-monsters exploring the deep. They saw, too, water monsters lying on the cliff slopes like those which often take the sorrowful journey in the morning over the sail-road, serpents and wild beasts. They rushed away, bitter and enraged; they had heard the noise, the song of the war horn. The Geatish chief cut one off from life, from its struggle in the waves, with a shaft from the bow. The hard war arrow stuck in its vitals; it was slower at swimming in the water; death carried it off. Quickly it was hard pressed by barbed boarspears on the waves, attacked by force, and dragged on to the cliff, a wondrous wave-roamer. The warriors looked on the horrible enemy.

Beowulf arrayed himself in princely garments; in no way did he fear for his life. His battle-corslet, hand-woven, ample and skilfully decorated, was to make trial of the lake. It could protect the body, so that the hostile grasp, the malicious grip of the enraged creature could not injure his breast or his life. The shining helmet protected the head of him who was to stir up the depths of the lake, seek the surging water. It was adorned with gold, encircled with splendid bands, as in days of old the weapon-smith fashioned it, decorated it with boar images, so that after-wards no sword or battle knife could bite into it. That was not the least of powerful aids which Hrothgar's spokesman lent him in his need: Hrunting was the name of that hilted sword. It was one of the foremost of ancient heirlooms. The blade was iron, stained with poisonous twigs, hardened by blood shed in battle. It had never failed any man in the fight, those who grasped it in their hands, who dared to enter into perilous expeditions, the meeting place of foes. It was not the first time that it was to perform deeds of valour. Surely, when he lent the weapon to a better swordsman, the son of Ecglaf, powerful and strong, did not remember what he had said before when drunk with wine. He himself dared not risk his life under the tumult of the waves, perform brave deeds. On this account he lost fame, renown for bravery. The other warrior was not like him after he had pre-pared himself for the fight.

Beowulf, the son of Ecgtheow, spoke: 'Remember now, Healfdene's famous son, wise prince, generous friend of men, now that I am ready for the mission, what we spoke of before. If I should lose my life in helping you in your need, you should always be in a father's place to me when I am dead; be a guardian to my retainers, my close companions, if battle carries me off. Also, beloved Hrothgar, send to Hygelac the treasures which you gave me. The lord of the Geats can then perceive from that gold, the son of Hrethel see, when he looks on that treasure, that I found a good ring-giver, enjoyed his generosity while I could. And may you, Unferth, the widely known man, have the ancient heirloom, the wondrous hard-edged sword with wavy orna-mentation. Either I will gain glory with Hrunting, or death will carry me off.'

After these words, the chief of the Geats pressed on bravely;

he did not wait for an answer. The surging water received the warrior. A good part of the day passed by before he could perceive the bottom. Immediately she who had, fiercely ravenous, grim and greedy, occupied the watery region for fifty years, discovered that one of the mortals was there examining the dwelling of monsters from above. Then she grasped at him, seized the warrior with her terrible grip; yet she did not so soon wound his unharmed body. The corslet hedged him around outside, so that she could not penetrate the coat of mail, the linked armour, with her hateful fingers. Then the she-wolf of the sea, when she came to the bottom, carried the armoured prince to her dwelling in such a way that he could not wield his weapons, no matter how brave he was; but many weird creatures harassed him in the water, numerous sea beasts broke his coat of mail with their battle-tusks; monsters pursued him.

Then the brave man realised that he was within some kind of hostile hall or other, where no water harmed him in any way, and the sudden rush of the flood could not touch him because of the roof of the hall. He saw a light from a fire, a brilliant flame shining brightly. Then the good man perceived the accursed monster of the deep, the powerful lake woman. He gave a mighty blow with his war sword; his hand did not hold back from the stroke, so that the patterned blade sang out a fierce battle song on her head. Then the attacker discovered that the shining sword would not cut, or do any injury; the blade failed the noble in his time of need. In times gone by it had survived many battles, cleft many a helmet, the corslet of a doomed man. It was the first time the precious treasure's power had failed.

Hygelac's kinsman was still resolute; his mind was set on glory; his courage did not lessen. Then the enraged warrior threw aside the sword covered with adornments and curved markings, so that it lay on the ground, strong and steel-edged. He put his trust in his strength, his powerful grip. So must a man behave when he wishes to win lasting fame in battle. He will have no concern for his life. The lord of the War-Geats seized Grendel's mother by the shoulder—he was not troubled by the conflict. Then the warrior brave in combat, inflamed with rage, flung the deadly enemy so that she fell to the ground. Immediately afterwards she gave him recompense and clutched at him with her savage claws. Then with a weary heart the strongest of warriors and foot soldiers stumbled and fell. Then she threw herself on the stranger in her hall and unsheathed her broad bright-edged dagger. She intended to avenge her son, her only offspring. The woven breast mail lay upon his shoulder; it was this that saved his life, prevented the entry of point and edge. The son of Ecgtheow, the champion of the Geats, would then have perished under the wide earth, had not his strong coat of mail helped him out. And the holy Lord, wise God, the Ruler of the heavens, brought about triumph in battle and with ease decided it rightly after the hero got to his feet again.

Then he saw in the fight a sword blessed with victory, an ancient blade made by giants, strong-edged, the glory of warriors; it was the best of weapons. However, it was too large for any other man to carry into battle, strong and splendid, the handiwork of giants. The hero of the Scyldings, fierce and savage, seized the ornamented hilt, drew the blade with curved designs, struck out furiously without a thought for his safety, so that it cut deeply into her neck, broke the bone. The sword went right through the body doomed to die. She fell to the floor; the sword was drenched with blood; the warrior rejoiced in his deed.

A gleam shone out; a light rose up in the hall just as the candle of the sky, the sun, shines brightly from heaven. Then he gazed about the hall, turned along the wall; Hygelac's thane, angry and resolute, raised his weapon firmly by the hilt. Its blade was not useless to the warrior, but he quickly wished to repay Grendel for the many raids which he had made on the West Danes, many more times than the one occasion when he slew Hrothgar's hearth-companions in their sleep, devoured fifteen Danes as they rested, and carried off as many more, loathsome plunder. The fierce warrior gave him his due for this, so that he saw Grendel lying at rest, weary after the battle, having lost his life, since he had been injured earlier in the fight at Heorot. The body gaped wide open when it suffered the blow, the savage sword stroke after death, and Beowulf cut off its head.

As soon as the wise men who watched the lake with Hrothgar saw that the surging water was all churned up, the water covered in blood, the grey-haired old men talked together about the brave warrior, saying that they did not expect the hero to return, to come back seeking the renowned prince, rejoicing in his victory. It seemed to many that the sea wolf had destroyed him. Then the ninth hour of the day came; the brave Scyldings left the headland; the generous friend of men went home. The Geatish strangers sat down, sick at heart, and gazed on the lake. They hoped, but did not expect, to see their lord and friend.

Then the sword, the war blade, began to fade away like icicles because of the blood of battle. It was a great marvel that it melted completely, just like ice when the Father, who controls seasons and times, loosens the bonds of frost, releases the fettered waters. He is the true Lord. The lord of the Weder Geats took no more treasures, although he saw many there, but only the head and the hilt adorned with jewels. The blade had completely melted; the damascened sword was burnt up, so hot was the blood and so venomous the hostile spirit that died there. The survivor of the conflict, the onslaught of enemies, was soon in the lake; he swam up through the water. The tossing waves, the spacious regions, were all purged when the terrible spirit relinquished its life and this transient world.

Then the guardian of seafarers came to land, swimming bravely; he rejoiced over the body he had won in the lake, the mighty burden which he had with him. Then the splendid band of retainers went to meet him; they thanked God, rejoiced that they could see their lord safe. Then the helmet and corslet were quickly taken from the valiant man. The lake, the water beneath the clouds, grew calm, stained with the blood of slaughter. They went onward from that place along foot-worn tracks with light hearts, traversed the paths, the well-known way. Men of kingly courage carried the head away from the lake-side slope with great difficulty for each of the brave warriors—four of them had great trouble in bearing Grendel's head on a spearshaft into the gold-hall.

At last the fourteen brave and distinguished Geats came

marching to the hall, and the lord of men, courageous in their midst, trod the level ground by the mead-hall. Then the chief of the thanes, a man of valiant deeds, gloriously exalted, a warrior brave in battle, entered to greet Hrothgar. Grendel's head was carried by the hair on to the floor where men drank, a fearful object before the nobles and the queen, a marvellous spectacle. Men gazed on it.

'THE BATTLE OF MALDON'

[The beginning and end are lost. The transcript (and presumably the destroyed Cottonian manuscript) begins as the English arrive at the field and prepare for battle.]

. . . was broken. Then he ordered each of the warriors to leave his horse, drive it afar, and advance on foot; to be intent on feats of arms and of steadfast courage. Then Offa's kinsman, upon perceiving that the earl [Byrhtnoth] would not tolerate slackness, let his beloved hawk fly from his hands away to the wood, and went forth to battle. By this it could be seen that the youth would not flag in the fight when he took up arms. Eadric also wished to serve his chief, his lord in battle; he proceeded to carry forth his spear to the fight. He had a dauntless spirit while in his hands he could hold shield and broadsword. He performed his vow that he would fight before his lord.

Then Byrhtnoth began to deploy his troops there. He instructed from horseback, directed the warriors how they should take up their positions and hold that place, and bade them hold their shields firmly upright with their hands, and have no fear. When he had deployed that force suitably, he dismounted among those people where he was most pleased to be, where he knew his most devoted household retainers were.

Then the Viking messenger stood on the shore and shouted sternly, spoke his words, he who threateningly delivered the seafarers' message to the earl as he stood on the land: 'Bold seamen sent me to you, commanded me to tell you that you must speedily send rings in return for peace; it is better for you to buy off this clash of spears with tribute than that we should join in bitter conflict. We need not slaughter each other if you are prosperous enough; we are willing to make a truce with that gold. If you who are of highest rank here will make the decision to ransom your people, pay to the seamen their choice of money in return for peace, and accept a truce from us, then we are ready to return to our ship with that tribute-money, put out to sea, and keep our peace with you.'

Byrhtnoth spoke; he raised his shield; brandished his slender spear; uttered words, wrathful and resolute gave him his answer: 'Seafarer, do you hear what this army says? Spears are the tribute they are prepared to pay you, deadly spear-point and trusty swords, war gear that will not profit you in battle. Messenger of the Vikings, carry this message back again; tell your people this more hateful news, that here stands a dauntless noble warrior with his war band, determined to defend this land of theirs, the country of Æthelred my lord, the people and the land. The heathens will fall in battle. It seems too shameful to me for you to board your ships with our tribute-money without a fight, since you have come so far here to our land. You will not carry off the treasure so easily; spear point and edge will first arbitrate between us, fierce battle-play, before we pay tribute.'

He bade the warriors take up their shields and advance so that they all stood on the river bank. But the water prevented the one troop from coming at the other; the flood tide came flowing after the ebb, and the incoming streams met round the island. It seemed too long to wait until they could bear their spears together. On each side of the River Panta [Blackwater] they stood in proud array, the battle line of Essex and the sea raiders, and none of them could harm the other unless anyone received death from the flight of an arrow.

The tide turned; the seamen stood ready, the Vikings longing for battle. The protector of heroes ordered a war-hardy warrior to hold the causeway—he was called Wulfstan—valiant as the stock from which he came. He was Ceola's son. With a throw of his spear he killed the first man who boldly stepped on to the causeway. There stood there with Wulfstan fearless fighters, Ælfere and Maccus, two brave men, who deigned to make flight at that ford; they steadfastly fought the foe while they still could wield their weapons. When they saw it and realised clearly that they found the bridge-guards fierce, then the hateful strangers began to resort to trickery, and asked that they should be allowed to land, to cross the ford, to lead their troops over.

Then out of proud overconfidence the earl proceeded to allow too much ground to the hateful host; Byrhtnoth, son of Byrht-helm, began to call over the chill, fateful water—the warriors listened: 'The way now lies open to you; come quickly to us, men to battle. Only God knows who shall be master of this field of battle.'

The warrior wolves of slaughter advanced; they took no heed of the water, the Viking war band. West across the Panta, across the shining water, they carried their shields, the men of the fleet bore their linden shields to land. There Byrhtnoth and his men stood ready against the foe. He bade them form a battle-hedge with their shields, and hold firm against the enemy war band. Then was the fight near, the hour of battle. The time was come when fated men must needs fall there. Then a clamour was raised; ravens wheeled, the eagle eager for carrion; there was uproar on the earth.

They sent forth spears from their hands, hard as the file; the cruelly ground spears flew; bows were busy: shield received spear-point. The battle was bitter: men fell on either side, young warriors lay dead. Wulfmær was wounded, Byrhtnoth's kins-man chose death in battle; he, his sister's son, was hewn down with swords. There the Vikings were given their requital: I heard that Eadward slew one with his sword; his hand did not stay the blow, so that the fated warrior fell at his feet. His lord gave him thanks for this, thanked his chamberlain when he had the chance. Thus the resolute young warriors stood firm in battle, eagerly considered who would first destroy with his spear-point the life of a fated man, of a warrior with weapons. The slain fell to the earth. They stood fast. Byrhtnoth exhorted them, bade that each warrior be intent on battle who wished to win glory fighting the Danes.

The stern man of battle advanced; he raised his weapon, his shield as protection, and went against a warrior. Thus the earl went in anger against a yeoman; each with evil intent for the other. Then the Viking sent a southern spear so that the lord of warriors was wounded. He struck with his shield so that the shaft broke, the spear shattered, and the head sprang away. The battle-warrior was enraged; with his spear he pierced the proud Viking who had given him the wound. He was an experienced soldier: he made his spear go through the man's neck; his hand so guided it that he deprived the sudden enemy of his life. Then he speedily struck a second blow so that his corslet burst; he was wounded in the breast through his chain mail; the deadly spear-point stood in his heart. The earl was the happier; the courageous man laughed; he thanked God for the day's work the Lord had given him.

Then one of the Viking warriors sent a spear from his hand, flying from his fist that it sped forth through Æthelred's noble thane. By his side stood a young warrior, not yet full grown, a youth in battle, Wulfstan's son, the young Wulfmær, who full valiantly drew the bloody spear out of the warrior's body; he sent the exceeding hard spear back again. The spear-point penetrated, and felled to the ground the man who had sorely pierced his lord. Then an armed man approached the earl; he wished to snatch his precious gear, his spoil, rings and orna-mented sword. Then Byrhtnoth drew his sword, broad and gleaming, from the sheath, and struck at his corslet. Quickly one of the seafarers prevented him and crippled the earl's arm; the golden-hilted sword fell to the ground, and he could not hold his hard blade, wield his weapon. Yet the hoary headed warrior still spoke these words; encouraged the young troops, bade them advance stoutly together. Then he could no longer stand firmly on his feet; he looked up to heaven: 'I give you thanks, Ruler of the people, for all the benefits of this world. Now, gentle Lord, I have great need for you to grant my soul joy, allow my spirit to journey to you, Lord of the angels, travel with peace into your keeping. I beseech you that the fiends of hell may do it no harm.' Then the heathen retainers hewed at him, and both the warriors who stood at his side, Ælfnoth and Wulfmær, lay slain when they yielded up their lives beside their lord.

Then those who did not want to be there turned from the battle. Odda's sons were first to flee; Godric left the fight, and forsook that good man who had often given him a horse. He mounted the steed he owed his lord, on those trappings which it was not right to mount, and both his brothers galloped with him; Godwine and Godwig had no taste for battle, but went from the fight, and made for the wood; they fled to that place of safety and saved their lives, and more men than there was any right to be if they had all kept in mind the favours which he had done them for their benefit. Offa said as much to him one day at the meeting place when he held a council, that many spoke out boldly there who afterwards in the hour of need would not endure.

Then the commander of the army, Æthelred's earl, had fallen. All his household retainers saw that their lord lay slain. The proud thanes advanced, the undaunted men hastened eagerly; all had one of two desires: to lay down their lives or to avenge their loved one. Thus the son of Ælfric encouraged them onward; the warrior young in years uttered these words; Ælfwine then spoke out valiantly: 'Remember those speeches which we often made over the mead, when we uttered loud boasts on the benches, warriors in hall boasting about stern combat. Now may a man prove how valiant he is. I will declare my lineage to all: that I am of a mighty family in Mercia; my grandfather was called Ealhelm, a wise earl, and prosperous in this world. Thanes among that people shall not reproach me because I wished to depart from this army, seek my native land, now that my chief lies hewn down in the battle. This to me is the greatest of griefs: that he was my kinsman and my lord.' Then he advanced; thought of battle so that he pierced one of the Vikings from that army with his spear-point so that he lay on the ground killed by that weapon. He then began to urge on his comrades, his friends and fellow-fighters to advance.

Offa spoke; he brandished his ashen spear: 'Behold, Ælfwine, you have encouraged all the thanes in our time of need. Now that our earl lies on the earth, we all have need to urge each other on, warriors to the fight, as long as he can retain and hold his weapon, the hard blade, the spear, and good sword. Godric, the cowardly son of Odda, has betrayed us all. A multitude of men believed when he rode on horseback on that splendid steed that it was our lord. And so here on the field of battle the army has split, the shield-wall shattered. May what he has done come to naught for putting so many men to flight here.'

Leofsunu spoke, and raised his shield, his shield as protection; he addressed the warrior: 'I tell you truly that I will not flee a footstep hence, but will advance further; avenge my lord and friend. Steadfast men from around Sturmere will have no cause to reproach me with words that when my patron has fallen I journey home without a lord, turn from the battle; instead a weapon shall have me, spear-point or iron blade.' Full of wrath he advanced, fought firmly; he scorned flight.

Dunnere then spoke; he brandished his spear; the plain yeoman called out after them all, bade that each of the warriors should avenge Byrhtnoth: 'He who among the host intends to take vengeance cannot flinch or value his life.'

Then they advanced; they took no thought for their lives. The household retainers began to fight grimly, the fierce spearmen, and prayed to God that they might avenge their friend and lord, and wreak slaughter on the foe. The hostage began to help them readily. He was the son of Ecglaf, of the bold Northumbrian race; his name was Æscferth. He never drew back from the fray, but often shot forth his arrows. Sometimes he pierced a shield with his dart, sometimes he struck a soldier. Almost every moment he dealt out an injury for as long as he could wield his weapons.

Then Eadward the tall still stood in the battle line, ready and eager; he spoke boasting words that he would not retreat a foot's length of land, turn back from where his lord lay. He broke the shield-wall and fought the warriors until he had worthily avenged his generous lord on the seamen before he lay among the slain. So did Ætheric, the noble companion, Sibyrht's brother, eager and forward pressing, fight most resolutely, and many another cleft the hollow shields; the valiant men defended themselves. Shield rim burst; corslet sang a terrible song. Then in the battle

Offa struck the seafarer so that he fell to the earth, and there Gadd's kinsman sought the ground. Offa was swiftly cut down in the fight: yet he had accomplished what he had promised his lord when he vowed to his benefactor that they should both ride home safely into the stronghold, or both fall in the fight, die from wounds on the battle-field. He lay, as befits a thane, close to his lord.

Then there was a shattering of shields; the Vikings advanced, engaged battle. Often spear pierced a fated body, the house of life. Then Wistan, the son of Thurstan, advanced, fought with the men. In the crush he slew three of them before Wighelm's son was slain. There was a stubborn conflict. The troops stood fast in the battle; warriors perished, wound-weary. The slain fell to the ground. Oswold and Eadwold, brothers both, exhorted the warriors all the while, with their words begged their dear kinsmen to endure in the hour of need, use their weapons without weakening.

Byrhtwold spoke—he was an old retainer; he raised his shield, brandished his ashen spear; he exhorted the warriors full boldly: 'Our spirit will be the braver, heart the more valiant, and courage the greater as our strength grows less. Here lies our lord, a good man cut down in the dust. May he mourn for ever who now thinks of turning from this sword play. I am old in years; I will not go, but intend to lie beside my lord, the most beloved of men.'

So too Æthelgar's son, Godric, encouraged them all to battle. Often he sent his spear, his deadly weapon, flying at the Vikings. Thus he went out in the forefront of the army, hewed and smote until he fell in battle. (He was not that Godric who fled the fight.) . . .

[The rest of the poem is lost.]

'GENESIS B': THE STORY OF ADAM AND EVE

Then God's enemy began to make ready, eagerly put on his armour. He had a guileful spirit. He placed on his head the helmet which made its wearer invisible, secured it firmly, fastened it with clasps. He was skilled in speech, cunning in word. He sprang upward, swept through the gates of hell (he had a ruthless heart), soared through the air with evil intent, splitting the fire in two with devilish skill. He wished to deceive men, the Lord's followers, secretly by wicked deeds, mislead and corrupt them so that they gained God's hatred. Then by fiendish cunning he made his way to where on earth he found Adam, God's creation, ready together with his wife, the fairest of women, fashioned with wisdom so that they served well with good works, for the Creator of mankind had appointed them his followers.

Near them stood two trees which were laden with fruit, clothed with plenty, just as the Lord God, the high King of Heaven, placed them with his hands, that there the sons of men, every human being, might choose between good and evil, weal and woe. Their fruit was not alike! One was so pleasant, splendid and shining, lithe and lovely; that was the tree of life. Whoever ate that fruit might live for ever afterwards in the world so that from that time on old age or grievous illness could do him no harm, but he would long live in happiness for ever, enjoy the favour of the Heavenly King here on earth, and glory ordained in high heaven when he left this place. The other was completely black, dark and shadowy; it was the tree of death. It bore much bitterness. Each man who tasted the fruit from that tree would go about this world knowing both good and evil, must ever after live in torment with sweat and sorrows. Old age should deprive him of brave deeds, joys and power, and death would be his destiny. He would enjoy his life for a short time, then seek the darkest of lands, enveloped in fire, be in subjection to devils for a long time in the place where there are the greatest of all perils for man. The hostile one, the dark messenger of the devil, who struggled against the Lord, was well aware of this.

Then he assumed the form of a snake and coiled himself around the tree of death with a devil's skill, took some of its fruit, and thence made his way to where he knew was the handiwork of the heavenly King. Then the hateful creature with his first words began to question him with lies: 'Adam, do you desire anything from God? I have journeyed here from afar on his errand; it is not long since I sat with him. He commanded me to take this journey, ordered you to eat this fruit; said that your strength and skill and spirit would grow greater and your body more beautiful, your form more splendid, said that you would lack no possessions in the world when you have fulfilled the wish, gained the good-will of the King of Heaven, served your Master to his satisfaction, made yourself dear to the Lord. I heard him praise your deeds and words in his splendour, and speak of your life. So you shall obey the commands which his messengers bring to this land. There are green realms far and wide in the world and God sits in the most exalted kingdom of heaven, the Almighty on high. The Lord of men does not want the trouble of making this journey himself, but he sends his follower to speak with you. Now he commands you in this lesson to learn to acquire skill. Eagerly perform his service; take this fruit in your hand, bite it and eat. Your mind will be keener, your body more beautiful. The Lord God, your Master, has sent you this from heaven as a help.'

Adam, a man not born of woman, spoke as he stood on earth: 'I heard the victorious Lord, Mighty God, speak with resounding voice, and he bade me remain here, keep his commandments; he gave me this wife, this beautiful woman, and bade me take care that I should not be tempted by the tree of death, grievously led astray. He said that whoever committed any evil in his heart would dwell in dark hell. I do not know whether you come here with lies and evil intent, or whether you are God's messenger from heaven. Lo! I cannot understand any of your biddings, your words or your ways, your journey or speeches. I do know what he, our Saviour, commanded me when I saw him last. He ordered me to honour his word, observe it well, obey his teaching. You are not like any of his angels whom I have seen before, nor do you show any sign which my Master graciously sent me as a pledge. For this reason I cannot obey you; you may go away. I have a firm belief in Almighty God who created me here by the power of his arms and hands. From his high kingdom he can endow me with every blessing without sending a messenger.'

With an enraged heart he turned to the place where he saw the woman, Eve, created in splendour, standing in the earthly kingdom. He said that the greatest of evils would afterwards fall on all their sons on earth. 'I know that God Almighty will be angry with you two when I return to him from the distant journey, and deliver the message that you refuse to obey his command that he sends here from the east on this occasion. Now he will come himself in response to your answer. His messenger cannot tell you his bidding. Therefore I know that he who is mighty in spirit will be angry with you. However, woman, if you willingly will heed my words, you may be freer to consider his counsel. Consider in your heart that you could avert punishment for you both with my advice. Eat this fruit. Then your eyes will become so clear that you will thereafter be able to see widely over the whole world and even the throne of your Master, and always enjoy his favour. Afterwards you can advise Adam, if you have his goodwill and he trusts your words. If you tell him truly what thoughts you have in your heart so that you carry out the command of God, then he will abandon the hostile strife, the wicked answer in his breast, if we talk to him for his good. Urge him eagerly to follow your advice, lest the two of you become hateful to God, your Ruler. If you carry out that enterprise, best of women, I will conceal from your Lord that Adam insulted me so much, spoke so many evil words. He accused me of untruths, said that I am a messenger eager to do cruel harm, and not an angel of God. I know very well the nature of the angels, the high vaults of heaven. So long was it that I zealously served God with a loyal spirit, my own high Lord. I am not like a devil.'

So he led her on with lies and trickery, with guile persuaded the woman into wrong-doing until the serpent's suggestion began to stir within her—the Creator had assigned her a weaker mind—so that she began to turn her thoughts to the temptation. Therefore she took the the noxious fruit from the tree of death, from the evil one, against the Lord's command. No worse deed has been decreed for mankind. It is a great wonder that eternal God would ever allow so many people who sought instruction to be misled by lies. Then she ate the fruit and broke the command and wish of the Almighty. Then she could see widely by the gift of a fiend who betrayed her with lies, deceived her secretly, through whose acts it seemed to her that heaven and earth were more fair, and all this world more beautiful, and God's creation vast and powerful, although she did not see it through man's counsel. Instead the foe who granted her sight that she might gaze on the kingdom of heaven first beguiled her soul.

Then the reprobate one spoke in enmity (he taught her nothing to her advantage): 'Now you may see for yourself, as I have no need to tell you, good Eve, that beauty and forms are not the same to you since you put your trust in my advice, obeyed my teaching. Now the light which I brought from God shines brightly over you, shining out of heaven. Now you can touch it. Tell Adam what power of sight you have acquired. If even now through modest conduct he follows my advice, then I will give him abundant light, just as I have granted you this good thing. I do not blame him for the wrong words, though he does not deserve forgiveness because of the many insults he spoke to me. So shall his own sons live afterwards; when they do wrong, they shall gain love, make amends for blasphemy and enjoy his goodwill from then on.'

Then the fairest of women went to Adam, the most beautiful of wives who came into the world because she was the handiwork of the Heavenly King, although she was then secretly corrupted, misguided by deceit in order that they would gain disfavour through the will of the adversary, through the devil's cunning forsake glory and the favour of their Master, be deprived of the kingdom of heaven for a long while. Then many men will be sorrowful that they did not keep their guard when they had the power. She carried one in her hand, the others lay at her heart, the cursed apple, the fruit from the tree of death, which formerly the Lord of Lords denied her. The Prince of Glory gave that command so that men, his subjects, need not suffer powerful death; instead the holy Lord gave the kingdom of heaven to all his people, enormous wealth, on condition that they would leave alone that one fruit, filled with bitterness, which the hateful tree bore on its branches; it was the tree of death which the Lord forbade them. He who was God's enemy, hateful to the Heavenly King, deceived them with lies, and Eve's heart, the weak mind of the woman, so that she put her trust in his words, followed his advice, believed that the counsel he so carefully explained to her came from God. He showed her a sign and gave his promise, his loyal intent.

Then she spoke to her master: 'Adam, my lord, this fruit is so sweet, so pleasant in the heart, and this messenger so fair, the good angel from God; I see from his appearance that he is the envoy of our Master, the King of Heaven. It is better that we gain his favour than his enmity. If today you insulted him in any way, he will even forgive it, if we do him homage. What good will such a hostile feud with our Master's envoy do you? We need his goodwill; he may take news of us to the Almighty, the King of Heaven. I can see from here where he sits in splendour—it is to the south-east—he who created the world. I see his angels wheel about him on their feathery wings, the greatest of all peoples, most lovely of hosts. Who could give me such knowledge, if God, the Ruler of Heaven, did not send it directly to me? I can hear far and wide, and see so clearly all the world over, this vast universe. I can hear the celestial rejoicing in heaven. Such clarity has been inside and outside my mind since I ate the fruit. Now, my good lord, I have it here in my hand; I would gladly give it you. I believe that it comes from God, brought by his command, as this messenger told me with well-chosen words. It resembles nothing else on earth unless, as the messenger says, it comes directly from God.'

She spoke to him often and all day urged him on to that dark deed, that they should break the Lord's command. The hateful messenger stood by, incited desires in them, persuaded them with deceit, pursued them boldly. Very near was the fiend who had made that daring journey over a long distance. He planned to cast mankind into mighty ruin, corrupt and mislead, so that they should lose the reward of God, the gift of the Almighty, possession of the heavenly kingdom. Lo, the enemy from hell knew very well that they would incur God's anger, and torment in hell, be obliged to endure terrible affliction after they had broken God's command, when he misled with lying words the beautiful woman, fairest of wives, to that wicked deed, so that she spoke according to his desire. God's own creation provided him with help in enticing them to sin.

Then the most beautiful of women spoke time and again to Adam until the man's mind began to be influenced so that he trusted in the promise that the woman told him about. Yet she did this with a loyal heart, and did not realise that so many sufferings, fearful affliction, would ensue for mankind, when she took to heart the promptings which she heard from the evil messenger. Instead she thought that she was gaining the favour of the King of Heaven with those words, when she showed the man such a token, and gave her promise until Adam's resolve changed within his breast, and his heart began to turn to her will. From that woman he received hell and death, though it was not so called, but it was to have the name of the fruit. Yet it was the sleep of death, the devil's artifice, hell and death, and destruction of men, the ruin of mankind, that they took as food, an evil fruit. So it came within him, touched at his heart.

Then the messenger with bitter intent laughed and danced, gave thanks to his lord for the two: 'Now I have gained your favour decreed for me, and carried out your desire for many days. Mankind is led astray, Adam and Eve. The displeasure of the Ruler is ordained for them, now that they have neglected his words and his teaching. Therefore they can no longer possess the kingdom of heaven, but they must go to hell on a dark journey. So you have no need to grieve for him in your breast where you lie in bondage, nor mourn in your heart that there are men dwelling in high heaven, while we now suffer afflictions, the misery of hell, a land of darkness. And through your mighty mind many have forsaken the high mansions in the kingdom of heaven, the gracious dwellings. God grew angry with us because we would not bow in subjection to the holy Lord in the heavenly realm. It did not suit us to serve him in allegiance. Therefore the Lord's mind was filled with rage towards us, stern in thought, and he drove us into hell, hurled the greatest race into that fire, and with his hands restored the celestial seats in heaven, and gave that kingdom to mankind. Your spirit can rejoice within your breast because here both plans have been accomplished: that the sons of men, mankind, should forsake the kingdom of heaven, and turn to you, burning, into that fire; and also that affliction and sorrow has been dealt out to God. Whatever torment we suffer here, it is now repaid to Adam by the hatred of the Master, and the ruin of man, and to men with the pangs of death. Therefore my mind is healed, the thoughts about my heart are relieved, all our afflictions, the sufferings that we have long endured, are avenged. Now I will again approach the flame, seek Satan there. He is in the darkness of hell bound in chain fetters.'

The most bitter messenger descended again; he was to seek the far-reaching fires and the gates of hell, where his master lay tied in chains. Adam and Eve were both sorrowful. They feared God, the displeasure of the Lord, greatly dreaded the enmity of the Heavenly King. They knew that they had resisted the commandments of God. The woman grieved, lamented with a sad heart (she had abandoned God's favour and teaching) when she saw that light fade, which the messenger through deceit had revealed to her, that they might endure the misery of hell, countless torments. Therefore sorrows burned in their breasts. Sometimes they fell in prayer, man and wife together, praised the victorious Lord, and called to God, the Ruler of Hell, and begged him that they might have his punishment, that they might willingly endure it, now that they had broken God's commandment. They saw that their bodies were bare; as yet they had no permanent dwelling in the land, nor did they know of the sorrows of work; but they could have lived well in the land if they had always followed the teaching of God. Then they spoke many words of sorrow together, both man and wife.

Adam spoke to Eve, and said: 'Lo! you, Eve, have brought this evil fate upon us. Now you see dark hell, ravenous and mighty. The kingdom of heaven is not like that fire; rather it is the best of lands, which we might have possessed with the grace of Our Lord, had you not listened to him who advised us to do this wrong. Thus we broke the word of the Ruler, the King of Heaven. Now we can lament this incident in misery. For he himself bade us be on our guard against sin, the greatest of afflictions. Now hunger and thirst cruelly tear at my breast; we have always before been untroubled by both. Now how shall we live, or dwell in this land if the wind comes from west or east, south or north? If clouds rise up, a hail shower comes driving down from heaven, if frost comes in the midst bringing chill to men. Sometimes this bright sun shines down with great heat, gleams over heaven, and we stand here naked, unprotected by garments. We have nothing by us for defence against storms, nor store set aside for food, and the Mighty God, the Ruler, is enraged with us. What will become of us now? Now I can repent that I prayed to the God of Heaven, the Good Ruler, to create you here for me from my limbs, since you have led me astray into the Master's displeasure. So for the rest of my life I may regret that I ever set eyes on you.'

Then Eve replied, the most splendid woman, most beautiful of wives; she was the work of God, though she was deceived by the devil's cunning: 'My friend Adam, you may blame me for it with your words; but you cannot grieve more bitterly in your mind than I do in my heart.'

Then Adam answered her: 'If I knew the will of the Lord, and what punishment I was to have from him you would see no one more ready than I, even though the God of Heaven command me to go hence on the sea, travel on the ocean. It would not be so deep or the sea so wide that I would falter. I would go to its depth if I could carry out God's will. Now I have no desire for any service on earth, now that I have lost my Lord's favour, so I may no longer enjoy it. But we must not go naked together. Let us go into this wood, into the protection of this forest.'

Then they both turned, grieving they went into the green wood, sat apart, awaiting the decree of Heaven's King himself, when they could no longer possess what the Almighty God gave them. Then they covered their bodies with leaves, clothed themselves with foliage—they had no proper garments. But they both fell down in prayer together every morning, begged the Mighty One that God Almighty should not forget them, and the Good Lord guide them thenceforth to live in the light.

'THE DREAM OF THE ROOD'

Lo! I will relate a marvellous dream which came to me in the middle of the night when men were at rest. It seemed to me that I saw a wondrous tree rising aloft, enveloped in light, the brightest of crosses. The whole of that sign was covered with gold, jewels gleamed at the surface of the ground, and there were five gems up on the cross-bar as well. The host of angels, beautiful by ancient decree, looked on there. Certainly this was no cross of evil. But holy spirits, men throughout the earth, and all this glorious creation, gazed on him there. The cross of victory was wondrous, and I stained with sin, sorely afflicted with wrong. I saw the tree of glory, adorned with hangings, shining beautifully, decked with gold. The Lord's tree was magnificently covered with gold. Yet, through that gold, I could discern the former agony of wretched men, that it had bled on the right side. I was greatly troubled with sorrows; I was afraid because of the beautiful vision. I saw that brilliant sign change colour and adornments: sometimes it was bedewed with moisture, drenched with flowing blood, sometimes it was gold-adorned.

And I, lying there a long time, looked on the Saviour's cross with troubled mind, until I heard it speak; the noblest tree began to utter words: 'It was years ago—I still remember it—that I was cut down at the edge of the forest, removed from my roots. Then strong and wicked men took me away, fashioned me as a spectacle for them, commanded me to raise up their criminals. Men carried me on their shoulders, until they set me on a hill; many foes secured me there. I saw the Lord of mankind making great haste in order to mount me. Then I dared not bend or break against the Lord's command when I saw the earth's surface shake. I could have struck down all the wicked men; yet I stood firm. Then the young Hero—who was God Almighty—strong and steadfast, took off his clothes. Brave in the sight of many, he climbed on the high cross, for he wished to redeem mankind. Then I trembled when the Hero clasped me; yet I dared not bend to the earth, fall to the ground, but I must stand firm.

'I was raised up as a cross; I supported the great King, the Lord of Heaven; I dared not bow. They pierced me through with dark nails; the scars are plain to see on me, open wounds of malice. I dared not harm any of them. They reviled us both together. I was completely drenched in blood, shed from the man's side after he had given up his spirit. I have suffered many harsh trials on the hill. I saw the God of Hosts cruelly stretched out. Darkness had covered the Lord's body, the bright radiance with clouds; shadows went forth, dark under the clouds. All creation wept, lamented the fall of the King. Christ was on the cross.

'Yet people came hastening from afar to the Prince. I saw it all. I was grievously afflicted with sorrows, yet I bowed to the men's hands humbly and willingly. Then they took Almighty God, lifted him down from the terrible torment. The warriors left me standing drenched with blood; I was severely injured with spear wounds. Then they laid him down, with weary limbs, stood by his head and looked on the Lord of Heaven, and he rested there for a time, exhausted after the great struggle. Then in the sight of the slayers men began to fashion him a tomb, carved it out of bright stone; they placed the triumphant Lord within. Then wretchedly in the eventime they began to sing a dirge when they were about to depart weary from the Great Lord; he rested there alone. Yet for a long time we stood there in our place, weeping after the voice of warriors had risen up. The corpse, the fair body, grew cold. Then men began to cut us down to the ground; that was a terrible fate. We were buried in a deep pit. Nevertheless the Lord's disciples, his friends, discovered me, decked me with gold and silver.

'Now beloved man, you may understand that I have endured the deeds of wicked men, grievous sorrows. Now that time has come that men honour me far and wide throughout the earth, and all this glorious universe prays to this sign. The Son of God suffered on me for a time; therefore now I tower gloriously under the heavens, and I may heal all those who fear me. Long ago I suffered the cruellest of torments, most hateful to men, before I revealed to mankind the true way of life. Lo! the Prince of Glory, the heavenly Lord, honoured me then above all the trees in the forest, just as he honoured his mother Mary herself above all womankind.

'Now I command you, dear man, to tell men of this sight, explain with words that it is the cross of glory on which God suffered for the many sins of mankind, and the deeds of old committed by Adam. There he tasted death; yet the Lord rose again by his great power to help men. Then he ascended into heaven; he will come here again in this world to visit mankind on the Day of Judgement, the Lord Himself, Almighty God, with his angels. Then he who has the power to judge will give judgement to each one as he formerly earned it here in this transitory life. No one can be unafraid of the word which the Lord utters. Before the multitude he will ask for the man who would taste bitter death for the sake of the Lord's name, as he did long ago on the cross. But then they will be afraid, and think little of what they began to say to Christ. He who once bore the best of signs in his breast need in no way be afraid; each soul that wishes to dwell with the Lord must through the cross seek a kingdom far from earth.'

I venerated the cross where I was alone without company. My spirit was anxious to depart. I felt many yearnings within me. Resorting to the cross is the joy of my life, now that I am able to visit it alone more than any other man, give it greater honour. Great is the desire for that in my heart, and I look to the cross for protection; I have not many powerful friends on earth. They have gone far from here, far from the joys of the world, have sought the King of Glory; now they dwell in heaven with the Father, live in glory. And every day I hope for the time when the Lord's cross, which I formerly beheld here on earth, will fetch me from this fleeting life, and bring me to the place where there is great happiness, joy in heaven, where God's people are seated at the feast, where there is perpetual bliss; then he will place me where I may thereafter dwell in glory, enjoy great joy with the saints. May the Lord who has suffered here on earth on the cross for men's sins befriend me. He redeemed us and gave us life and home in heaven.

Hope is renewed with blessings and with joy to those who endured burning there. The Son was victorious on his journey [i.e., the Harrowing of Hell], powerful and successful. Then he came with a multitude, a host of spirits into the kingdom of God, the Almighty Lord to the joy of the angels and all the saints who before lived in heaven in glory when their Lord Almighty came to where his home was.

'THE WANDERER'

'The solitary man often prays for mercy, the Creator's kindness; though sad at heart he must long row the rime-cold sea, wander in exile. His fate cannot be changed.'

Thus spoke the Wanderer remembering hardships, cruel slaughter, the loss of kinsmen: 'Often must I each dawn bewail my sorrow in solitude; there is now no man alive to whom I dare clearly open my thoughts. I know only too well that it is a wholesome habit for a man to bind his heart fast, to hold his tongue, no matter what he thinks. A weary heart cannot fight against its fate, nor can sad thoughts afford comfort. Therefore those who are eager for glory often keep their sad thoughts fast in their breast.

'So, worn out by cares, cut off from my native land and from my kinsmen, I often had to fetter my thoughts, when in years gone by the darkness of the earth covered my generous lord, and I went thence in misery with wintry care over the frozen waves, and in sorrow looked for the hall of a dispenser of treasure, wherever I could find him near or far who would acknowledge me in the mead-hall, succour me who had no friends, entice me with pleasures.

'He who has had experience knows how cruel a companion sorrow is for the man who has few dear protectors. Exile is his lot, never braided gold; a chill heart, never earth's riches. He remembers the retainers in hall, the treasure he received, how in his youth his generous lord feasted him; all joy has perished. And so he who must long forgo his beloved lord's advice knows this when sorrow and sleep come together to chain the unfortunate solitary; in his mind's eye he seems to be clasping and kissing the lord of men, laying his hand and head in his lord's lap as when once of old he used to enjoy the gift-throne. Then the friendless man awakes again and sees the dark waves before him, the sea birds bathing and spreading their feathers, the frost and snow falling with hail between. Then his heart's wounds are the heavier, the grief for his dear lord; his sorrow is renewed.

'Then the remembrance of kinsmen goes through his mind; he greets them with joy, dwells on them eagerly. The companions of men swim back on their way; the images of sailors do not bring much familiar speech there. Care is renewed in him who must continually cast his weary mind over the frozen waves. And so I cannot think why my heart is not clouded in this world when I call to mind all the life of great men: how they suddenly relinquished the hall, brave retainers. Thus this earth of ours daily slips and falls.

'Therefore no man can become wise until he has had his share of winters in this world. A wise man must be patient, not over hot-headed or hasty of speech; not too fearful, glad or greedy; never too prone to boasting before he knows all. A man should wait when he utters a boast until in his pride he knows well the thoughts of his heart will turn.

'The wise man must perceive how strange it will be when all the wealth of this world stands waste, as now in various places in the land walls stand blown upon by winds, covered with hoar frost, the dwellings in ruins. Wine-halls crumble; their rulers lie dead, deprived of joy; the whole retainer-band has fallen proud by the wall. Some battle took, carried them away; one a bird bore off over the high sea; one the grey wolf gave over to death; one a sad-faced earl hid in an earth-cave. The Creator of men laid this earth waste so that the old work of giants stood empty without the townsfolk's revelry.

'He who has wisely considered these foundations and thought deeply about this dark life, old in heart calls to mind from far-off days the multitude of slaughter, and speaks these words: 'Where has the horse gone, where the man, where the treasure giver? Where has the banquet hall gone? Where are the joys of the feast? Alas the bright cup; alas the corsleted warrior, alas the prince's glory! How that time has passed, grown dark under night's helmet as if it had never been. There now stands where stood the warrior-band a wall, wondrous high, serpent-decorated. The might of ash spears has taken the earls, the weapon greedy for slaughter; their fate was glorious. Tempests beat against the stony slopes; the falling storm binds the earth, the uproar of winter. Then dark comes, night's shadows draw on, send forth fierce hail-storms from the north in hostility to man. All is hardship in earth's kingdom; the decrees of fate overthrow the world under the heavens. Here property passes away; here friends pass away; here men pass away; here kin pass away. The whole structure of the earth becomes desolate.'

Thus spoke the wise man in his heart; he sat apart musing. Good is he who keeps his faith; this man will never speak his anguish hastily from his heart, unless he first knows the remedy he can perform nobly. It is well for him to seek mercy, consolation from the Father in heaven, where for all of us our security is fixed.

'THE SEAFARER'

A true tale can I tell of myself, speak the truth: how I often in my days of toil suffered a time of hardship, endured bitter care in my heart, experienced on shipboard many an abode of care, the rough rolling of the waves. There the hardship of the night watch was often my lot in the ship's prow, while she tossed about by the cliffs. My feet were afflicted with cold, bound fast by frost with cold fetters; care then sighed hotly round my heart; hunger inside me tore at my sea-weary mind. A man who prospers ashore cannot know how I, worn with care, spent a winter on the ice-cold sea in the paths of an exile, deprived of loving kinsfolk, icicle-hung. Hail flew in showers; I heard nothing there except the resounding of the sea, the icy waves, and sometimes the cry of the swan. The clamour of gannets served for my pleasure, the cry of the curlew instead of the laughter of men; the sound of the sea-mew instead of the mead drink. There storms battered against the stony cliffs; there the tern answered icy-feathered; often the dewy-winged eagle screamed aloud. No protector was there to console the despairing mind. And so he who enjoys a happy life in the town and little hardship, proud and wine-flushed, little believes how I often weary at heart had to dwell on the sea ways. Night's shades grew dark; it snowed from the north; frost fettered the earth; hail fell on the ground, the coldest of seed corn.

So thoughts now jostle my heart that I should explore the deep streams, the play of the salt waves, myself; my mind's desire continually prompts my heart to set forth, so that far from here I may visit the country of strange people. There is no man upon earth so bold, so free of his gifts, so valiant in his youth, so brave in his deeds, with a lord so gracious to him that he has never felt anxiety for his sea journey about what the Lord would do to him. He cares not for the harp, for the receiving of rings, for pleasure in women, for worldly joy, for nothing but the rolling of the waves. Woods come into flower, cities become beautiful, fields grow fair, the world awakes; all this urges the heart of an eager man to a voyage, of him who intends to journey far on the ocean ways. The cuckoo with its sad voice also urges, the sign of summer sings, bodes bitter sorrow at heart. He does not know, the man who lives in luxury, what some suffer then for whom the paths of exile lie most open. My thoughts turn in my heart, my mind towards the sea, the home of whales, turns far and wide over the face of the earth, comes back to me eager and insatiable. The solitary flier screams, irresistibly whets the heart to the whale-road over the expanse of the ocean.

Therefore the joys of the Lord are warmer to me than this dead transient life on earth; I do not believe that earthly prosperity lasts for ever. Each of three things is doubtful until its time comes: sickness, age and violence may rob a doomed and fated man of his life. For this reason the praise of the living, spoken in later days, is the best posthumous fame for every man: that before he died he strove after earthly benefits, and accomplished brave deeds against the malice of enemies and the devil, so that the sons of men may praise him later, and his fame live for ever and ever with the angels, the glory of everlasting life, joy among the angel host.

Those days have departed, all the pomp of earthly kingdoms; there are now no kings, no emperors, no givers of gold now, as once there were, when they performed the greatest deeds of glory and lived in most lordly state. All this host has perished; joy is departed. Weaker men have succeeded them, and possess this world, enjoy it through their labour. Glory is laid low; earth's nobleness grows old and withers, as does every man throughout this earth of ours. Age comes upon him; his countenance turns pale; he mourns grey-haired; he knows his friends of old, sons of princes, have been consigned to the earth. Nor may his body, the house of flesh, when his life departs, swallow sweet things, nor suffer pain, nor raise an arm, nor think thoughts. Though his brother will spread his brother's grave with gold, lay him beside the dead with many a treasure, it will not go with him; nor can the gold, which he hid beforehand while he yet lived, help a sinful soul in the face of the dread judgement of God. Great is the fear of God; it alters the earth. He established the firm lands, the surface of the earth, and the sky above. He is a fool who does not fear his Lord; death will come to him unexpected. Happy is he who lives humbly; mercy will come to him from heaven. The Creator established that trait in him because he trusts in his strength.

A man should curb his headstrong heart, hold it firmly; be faithful among men; pure in his ways. Every man should bear himself with moderation towards friend and evil enemy, though he may wish for him his fill of fire, or has burned on the pyre his worthy lord. Fate is stronger, the Maker mightier than the mind of any man. Let us ponder where our home is, and then consider how we may come there, work it also that we may get to that eternal bliss where the love of the Lord is the fountain of life, joy in heaven. Thanks be to the Holy One, that he, the Prince of Glory, the eternal Lord, has thus honoured us, for ever and ever. Amen.

Further Reading

I. LEARNING THE LANGUAGE

It is possible to take one of the texts listed in Chapter 7, and to begin translating it word for word with the aid of the vocabulary—most texts have good vocabularies at the back. The first page will take hours rather than minutes, but the second will take less, and the third less than the second. A surer and in the long run faster way is to learn sufficient grammar to recognise the part of speech. For this purpose the best works are probably:

Mitchell, B., *A Guide to Old English*. 2nd ed. Blackwell, 1968.
Quirk, R. & Wrenn, C. L., *An Old English Grammar*. 2nd ed. Methuen, 1958. [Particularly good on syntax.]

Sweet's *Primer*, listed below, also has a grammatical outline.

2. READERS

There are a large number of anthologies of Old English texts available, and choice between them is largely a matter of personal preference. We have listed some of the more modern or more recently revised ones. Of these, Sweet's *Primer* has sufficient grammatical apparatus for a beginner, and Hamer's is confined to verse, but has a facing translation.

Fowler, R., *Old English Prose and Verse*. Routledge, 1966.
Hamer, R., *A Choice of Anglo-Saxon Verse*. Faber, 1970.
Sweet, H., *An Anglo-Saxon Primer, with Grammar, Notes and Glossary*. 9th ed., rev. N. Davis. Clarendon Press, 1953.
Sweet, H., *An Anglo-Saxon Reader in Prose and Verse*. 15th ed., rev. D. Whitelock. Clarendon Press, 1967.

3. COLLECTED TRANSLATIONS

The translations we list vary considerably in approach, style and cost. Alexander's is cheap and readily available, and is particularly valuable for his introductions to each poem and to the poetry in general. At the other extreme Gordon is reliable and more comprehensive than any other—he translates a lot of verse that other, more poetic translators despise—but his renderings are more pedestrian.

Alexander, M., *The Earliest English Poems*. Penguin, 1966.

Crossley-Holland, K., *The Battle of Maldon, and other Old English Poems*. Macmillan, 1970.

Crossley-Holland, K., *Storm, and other Old English Riddles*. Macmillan, 1970.

Gordon, R. K., *Anglo-Saxon Poetry*. 2nd ed. Everyman, 1954.

Kennedy, C. W., *An Anthology of Old English Poetry*. New York, O.U.P., 1960.

Kennedy, C. W., *Early English Christian Poetry*. New York, O.U.P., 1963.

4. STUDIES ON THE LANGUAGE

Baugh, A. C., *A History of the English Language*. 2nd ed. Routledge, 1959. [A standard conventional history of the language; *i.e.* it starts at the beginning.]

Chambers, R. W., *On the Continuity of English Prose*. E.E.T.S., 1932. [This extract from the introduction to his edition of Harpsfield's *Life of More* was an early example of the arguments for continuity between Old English and later periods, and is still worth a glance today.]

Clark, J. W., *Early English: a Study of Old and Middle English*. rev. ed. Deutsch, 1967.

Gordon, I. A., *The Movement of English Prose*. Longman, 1966. [An unusually well-written account of English prose style from the earliest times to the present.]

Strang, B. M. H., *A History of English*. Methuen, 1970. [In this unconventional history of the language Mrs. Strang begins with modern times and works backwards to the earliest period. The advantage is that by working from the known to the unknown the context for each new period has already been provided; the disadvantage for those interested only in the earliest period is that there is a lot to read first.]

5. GENERAL LITERARY HISTORY AND CRITICISM

Baugh, A. C. (ed.), *A Literary History of England*. 2nd ed. Routledge, 1967. [Also available in paperback in four separate parts. The relevant one is the first, but even so devotes only 100 out of 300 pages to our period.]

Bolton, W. F. (ed.), *The Middle Ages*. Barrie & Jenkins: Sphere, 1970.

Greenfield, S. B., *A Critical History of Old English Literature*. University of London Press, 1966. [Just what the title says.]

Ker, W. R., *Medieval English Literature*. Home Univ. Library, 1912, etc. [An old, but not outdated survey, by a scholar who has read more widely than many of his modern successors. Earlier editions have the title: *English Literature: Medieval*.]

Renwick, L. & Orton, H., *The Beginnings of English Literature to Skelton, 1509*. 3rd ed., rev. M. F. Wakelyn. Cresset Press, 1966. [Particularly valuable for the bibliographical chapter which follows the hundred-page introductory survey.)

Sampson, G., *The Concise Cambridge History of English Literature*. 3rd ed. C.U.P., 1970.

Stanley, E. G. (ed.), *Continuations and Beginnings*. Nelson, 1966. [A collection of valuable essays by various scholars; but read a more general book first.]

Wrenn, C. L., *A Study of Old English Literature*. Harrap, 1967. [The result of a philologist's lifetime study of the literature.]

6. HISTORY AND ART

Anglo-Saxon Illumination in Oxford Libraries. Bodleian Library, 1970. [A cheap pamphlet showing some of the finer pages from some of the finer manuscripts.]

Blair, P. H., *An Introduction to Anglo-Saxon England*. C.U.P., 1956. [A good all-round introduction.]

Brooke, C. N. L., *From Alfred to Henry III, 871–1272*. Nelson: Sphere, 1961.

Bruce Mitford, R. L. S., *The Sutton Hoo Ship Burial: a Handbook*. British Museum, 1968. [The official account for the general reader.]

English Historical Documents. Vol. 1. Eyre and Spottiswoode, 1955. [The earliest volume in a massive series presenting documents of importance to English History, translated in the case of this volume.]

Stenton, F. M., *Anglo-Saxon England.* 3rd. ed. Clarendon Press, 1971. [A standard history, fuller than most beginners will want.]

Talbot Rice, D. (ed.), *The Dark Ages: the Making of European Civilization.* Thames & Hudson, 1965. [A lot of splendid pictures.]

Whitelock, D., *The Beginnings of English Society.* Pelican, 1952. [Particularly good on the social aspects.]

Wilson, D. M., *The Anglo-Saxons.* Thames & Hudson, 1960. [Emphasis on art and archaeology.]

Index

Bold figures indicate major references; italic figures indicate quotations or translations.